# The Presence by Margaret Cavendish

Margaret Lucas Cavendish, Duchess of Newcastle-upon-Tyne was born in 1623 in Colchester, Essex into a family of comfortable means.

As the youngest of eight children she spent much time with her siblings. Margaret had no formal education but she did have access to scholarly libraries and tutors, although she later said the children paid little attention to the tutors, who were there 'rather for formality than benefit'.

From an early age Margaret was already assembling her thoughts for future works despite the then conditions of society that women did not partake in public authorship.  For England it was also a time of Civil War. The Royalists were being pushed back and Parliamentary forces were in the ascendancy.

Despite these obvious dangers, when Queen Henrietta Maria was in Oxford, Margaret asked her mother for permission to become one of her Ladies-in-waiting. She was accepted and, in 1644, accompanied the Queen into exile in France. This took her away from her family for the first time.

Despite living at the Court of the young King Louis XIV, life for the young Margaret was not what she expected. She was far from her home and her confidence had been replaced by shyness and difficulties fitting in to the grandeur of her surroundings and the eminence of her company.

Margaret told her mother she wanted to leave the Court. Her mother was adamant that she should stay and not disgrace herself by leaving.  She provided additional funds for her to make life easier.  Margaret remained.  It was now also that she met and married William Cavendish who, at the time, was the Marquis of Newcastle (and later Duke). He was also 30 years her senior and previously married with two children.

As Royalists, a return to life in England was not yet possible.  They would remain in exile in Paris, Rotterdam and Antwerp until the restoration of the crown in 1660 although Margaret was able to return for attention to some estate matters.

Along with her husband's brother, Sir Charles Cavendish, she travelled to England after having been told that her husband's estate (taken from him due to his being a royalist) was to be sold and that she, as his wife, would receive some benefit of the sale. She received nothing.  She left England to be with her husband again.

The couple were devoted to each other.  Margaret wrote that he was the only man she was ever in love with, loving him not for title, wealth or power, but for merit, justice, gratitude, duty, and fidelity.  She also relied upon him for support in her career. The marriage provided no children despite efforts made by her physician to overcome her inability to conceive.

Margaret's first book, 'Poems and Fancies', was published in 1653; it was a collection of poems, epistles and prose pieces which explores her philosophical, scientific and aesthetic ideas.

For a woman at this time writing and publishing were avenues they had great difficulty in pursuing. Added to this was Margaret's range of subjects. She wrote across a number of issues including gender, power, manners, scientific method, and philosophy.

She always claimed she had too much time on her hands and was therefore able to indulge her love of writing. As a playwright she produced many works although most are as closet dramas. (This is a play not intended to be performed onstage, but instead read by a solitary reader or perhaps out loud in a small group. For Margaret the rigours of exile, her gender and Cromwell's closing of the theatres mean this was her early vehicle of choice and, despite these handicaps, she became one of the most well-known playwrights in England)

Her utopian romance, 'The Blazing World', (1666) is one of the earliest examples of science fiction. Margaret also published extensively in natural philosophy and early modern science; at least a dozen books.

She was the first woman to attend a meeting at Royal Society of London in 1667 and she criticized and engaged with members and philosophers Thomas Hobbes, René Descartes, and Robert Boyle.

Margaret was always defended against any criticism by her husband and he also contributed to some of her works. She also gives him credit as her writing tutor.

Perhaps a little strangely she said her ambition despite her shyness, was to have everlasting fame. During her career, from the mid 1650's until her death, she was prolific. In recent decades her work has undergone a resurgence of interest propelled mainly by her ground-breaking attitude and accomplishments in those male straitened times.

Margaret Cavendish died on 15th December 1673 and was buried at Westminster Abbey.


# Index of Contents

As an Introduction to the Play.

Enter **TWO GENTLEMEN**.

**1ST GENTLEMAN**
Tom, How do you like the New
Plays?

**2ND GENTLEMAN**
As I like an Old Wife,
Not well.

**1ST GENTLEMAN**
If the judgment of the Stage should hear you, they would condemn you.

**2ND GENTLEMAN**
Faith, that Condemnation would be a Commendation to me, and a reproach to themselves; for those that cannot judge of Wit, cannot judge of Me.

**1ST GENTLEMAN**
Cannot they judg of Wit, say you?

**2ND GENTLEMAN**
No; for those that understand not Wit, cannot judge of Wit.

**1ST GENTLEMAN**
Do they not understand Wit?

**2ND GENTLEMAN**
No, for if they did, they would not applaud Plays, that have neither Humour, Wit, nor Satyr; which are those they name New Plays, made up of Old Romances.

**1ST GENTLEMAN**
But New Plays have Plots, Designs, Catastrophes and Intrigues.

**2ND GENTLEMAN**
What are those?

**1ST GENTLEMAN**
Those are to express Policy, Ingenuity and Art; besides, they describe Love, Justice, Honour, and the like.

**2ND GENTLEMAN**
Why, Seneca doth express Moral Virtues, and Machiavillian Policy, better and more properly then Dramatick Poetry; and the Spectators will learn more in one day by reading their Works, or such like Authors, then by seeing forty Plays, and less Charge: Besides, it doth lessen the esteem of such grave Learning, neither is it more proper for Plays then the Scripture is.

**1ST GENTLEMAN**
But the Scripture was Acted in the old time.

**2ND GENTLEMAN**
Truly, and I have heard they were foolish Plays, although made out of the Sacred Scripture; and that there was a Superscription of one Play set upon a Post, which was thus, Here is a Play to be seen of King Saul, with the merry Conceits of David and Goliah; which certainly was profane. But a Stage is not an University, Grammar-School, or Church; for by such actions or descriptions, it would rather abuse Religion, and corrupt Learning, then advance them; for though the Stage may be very beneficial to young persons to learn good Behaviour, Discourse and Wit, yet not to learn Morality and Divinity; and as for Policy, all Men are naturally apt to be Dissemblers, they shall not need to be instructed; also, concerning the description of foolish Romancical Love, it doth but corrupt the minds and thoughts of Men and Women, which causes not only foolish and unhappy Marriages, but wicked Adulteries.

**1ST GENTLEMAN**
But pray tell me what you mean by that you name Satyr? whether you do not mean railing?

**2ND GENTLEMAN**

No, for railing is to speak ill of particular persons; but Satyr is to reprove general Vices.

**1ST GENTLEMAN**
And what do you mean by Wit and Humour?

**2ND GENTLEMAN**
By Wit I mean similizing, and distinguishing of Words and Things; by Humour I mean the Behaviours, Dispositions and Practices of Mankind; all which good Comedies will inform Youth better, then far and dangerous Travels; but as for Morality and Policy, as I said before, they are more proper for Schools and States, then for Stages.

**1ST GENTLEMAN**
But Lovers Scenes are most pleasing to the
Spectators, and are the best part in a Play.

**2ND GENTLEMAN**
In my opinion the Lover's part is the worst part; but as for such Love-making as is in the New Plays, it would give me as good a vomit to see it, as Crocus Mettallorum steept in wine, or the like, and swallow'd down my throat.


SCENE II

[Enter as in the Presence, **MONSIEUR CONVERSANT, MONSIEUR OBSERVER**, and **MONSIEUR MODE**.

**CONVERSANT**
Good Morrow Gentlemen; Mons. Mode, did not you attend the Emperor to the Chappel to day?

**MODE**
No, but I am going to attend him from the
Chappel.

**CONVERSANT**
It had been better you had attended him into the Chappel for your own sake, for there you might have said your Prayers, which, it is probable, you Courtiers seldom do.

**MODE**
Faith, we Courtiers have little time to pray; for what with Dressing, Trimming, Waiting, Ushering, Watching, Courting, and the like, all our time is spent.

**OBSERVER**
It seems Courtiers are so much concern'd with their bodies, as they regard not their Souls.

**MODE**
Pleasure lives with the Body, and we Courtiers live with Pleasure; as for the Soul it is not well known what it is; but let it be what it will, or can be, or is, yet it belongs more to another World, then to this; which other World we Courtiers care not for, nor think thereof; we only desire to be happy in this

World, for we are well content to quit the Happiness of the next World for the pleasure of this present World.

**CONVERSANT**
But yet when Courtiers come to die, they will wish they had thought more of the next World, and less of this.

**MODE**
Faith, we Courtiers never think of Death, until Death think of us; and when Death remembers us so, as to take us out of this World, we believe we shall only die and turn to dust, and be no more; we are only troubled and grieved that our Masking delights are at an end, and that our light of life, and delights of Pleasures must be put out by Death's Exstinguisher; the truth is, with Court-Gallants, Court-Officers, and State-Magistrates, it is according to the old observation, which is, They live without Conscience, and die without fear.

**OBSERVER**
I did believe that Courtiers had been so vain, that they could not be so valiant, as to die without fear.

**MODE**
There are many sorts of Valours, or rather I may say, Courages; for though most Courtiers have not Valour to fight Duels, or in Battels; yet they have courage to run in debt, not fearing Imprisonment, and they have courage to Court Mistresses, not fearing the Pox; also, they have courage to flatter, cozen, dissemble, profess, protest, and then betray, not fearing dishonour.

**CONVERSANT**
Will not Courtiers fight, say you?

**MODE**
No faith, if they can chuse to avoid it; for we Courtiers are Men for life, and not for death; for though we are Men of Action, yet not Warlike Actions.

**CONVERSANT**
In what are Courtiers active?

**MODE**
In Dancing, Racing, Tennis-playing, Carding, Dicing, and the like; for should a Soldier become a Courtier, he would become a Coward in a short time; for the Pleasures of the Court do abate the Courage of War.

**CONVERSANT**
I believe you, because you are a Courtier, and know a Courtier best; but I fear you will not appear a diligent Attendant, if you go not to the Chappel to wait upon the Emperour.

**MODE**
You say true, wherefore farwell.

**CONVERSANT**
But before you go, pray inform us of the cause that makes the Princess so Melancholy?

**MODE**

That which makes most Women Melancholy, to wit, Amorous Love.

**OBSERVER**

'Tis said, that it is a pleasing pain; but is the Princess in Love?

**MODE**

Yes.

**CONVERSANT**

With whom?

**MODE**

With no body.

**CONVERSANT**

Can she be in Love with no body?

**MODE**

Yes faith, rather then Women, will not be in love, they will love no body.

**CONVERSANT**

That is impossible.

**MODE**

It is not impossible, if an Idea be no body; and 'tis said, Thoughts are Ideas.

**OBSERVER**

I suppose that no Women are in love with their own Thoughts, for if they were, they would think more, and speak less; wherefore, you are mistaken; for Women are in love with their own Words.

**MODE**

If they be, their love is placed still upon no body; for the old opinion is, That Words are bodiless: But the Princess is in love with an Idea she met with in a Dream in the Region of her Brain; and unless she may enjoy this Idea, not only awake, but imbodied, she cannot be at rest in her mind!

**CONVERSANT**

If this be true, it is a strange Love!

**MODE**

It is as true as strange, and as strange as true; and all the Ladies in the Court are become Dreaming-Lovers to imitate the Princess.

**OBSERVER**

All the Ladies, say you?

**MODE**

Yes faith, All, both Maids, Widows and Wives.

**CONVERSANT**
As for Wives, it is fit they should never have other Lovers, both for their Husbands and their own sake; for then their Love and Lovers cannot possibly be known, if they can but keep their own Counsels.

**MODE**
But they cannot keep their own Counsels, for if they could, they would never have divulged their Amorous Dreams.

[Exit **MODE**.

[Enter **SPEND-ALL** to **CONVERSANT** and **OBSERVER**.

**CONVERSANT**
Monsieur Spend-all, I wish you joy of your Preferment, for I hear you have a place bestow'd upon you, agreeable and proper for your Pastime and Profession; for you being a great Gamester, are made Croom-Porter.

**SPEND-ALL**
No faith, but I am not; for Keep-all, the old miserable Userer, is made Groom-Porter.

**CONVERSANT**
Why, that is very well; for he may put out his Money to use amongst the Gamesters, and have Am's ace for his Interest; but if he be made Groom-Porter, you shall be Lord Treasurer.

**SPEND-ALL**
No faith, I would have but one Office, if I might have my choice.

**OBSERVER**
What Office is that?

**SPEND-ALL**
Master of the Mint.

**OBSERVER**
That will not do you much good, unless you were Master of the Coyn; but if you were Master of the Coyn, you would play all away at Cards and Dice, Tennis, and such like Games.

**SPEND-ALL**
If I did, I should do but as most Gentlemen do, that have Estates, which spend their Money for their pleasure, and I take Pleasure in Gaming.

**CONVERSANT**
But not to lose.

**SPEND-ALL**
I had rather lose, then not play.

**OBSERVER**
I did believe that Gamesters play'd more out of covetousness, then for pleasure.

**SPEND-ALL**
You mistake; for Gamesters are more in love with Cards, Dice, and Rackets, then Lovers are with Women.

**CONVERSANT**
And I believe Gamesters fear Fortune more then Lovers do the Spiritual Court, the Parish-Constable, or the City-Watch.

**SPEND-ALL**
Faith, Fortune is like most Magistrates, or great Officers, who will cruelly punish some, and partially favour others; and all her actions are without Reason and Justice.

**OBSERVER**
But you cannot bribe Fortune.

**SPEND-ALL**
No, and in that respect Lovers have the better of Gamesters.

**CONVERSANT**
But Gamesters are for the most part Lovers.

**SPEND-ALL**
Faith, no; for a Gamester cannot spare so much time, as to kiss a Mistress; but fare you well, for I must go to the Porters Lodge.

**CONVERSANT**
But tell me truly, before you go, whether Keep-all the Usurer is made Groom-Porter?

**SPEND-ALL**
The truth is, I did but jest; for he is not
Groom-Porter, but the Knave of Clubs is made
Groom-Porter.

**CONVERSANT**
If it be so, then that place is properly served, for the Knave of Clubs is a fit person for that Office.

[Exeunt **MEN**.


SCENE III

[Enter the **PRINCESS** and her **GOVERNESS**.

**PRINCESS**

Which of the Gods and Goddesses shall I pray to assist me, since my beloved is Spiritual, and not Mortal, at least not Temporal; but yet he is not Coelestial; for surely an Idea is not a god, although it be not a bodily Creature?

**GOVERNESS**
But Souls may meet and converse, and enjoy each other.

**PRINCESS**
How meet?

**GOVERNESS**
In the Mind.

**PRINCESS**
But that's no satisfaction to Humane kind.

**GOVERNESS**
I know not whether Satisfaction doth, but surely Tranquility lives in the Mind; and the god of Dreams hath presented the Idea, which surely is the Soul of some Noble and Meritorious Lover, as a reward to your Vertue.

**PRINCESS**
How foolishly you talk! as if the gods were Lover's Mediators: But if they should humble themselves in such Amorous Imployments, and did present this Idea, then I should enjoy it every time I sleep; but alass, I never did perceive it but once, and then like as a Heavenly Vision, no sooner perceived, but vanished away.

**GOVERNESS**
But can you love so much upon so small an acquaintance?

**PRINCESS**
I am of Marlow 's opinion,
Who ever lov'd, that loves not at first sight!
But this Idea is fixed in my heart,
And whilst I live will never thence depart:
But I will make Apelles my dear Saint,
And he shall both my Love and Passion paint.
Apelles, draw this Passion in my Heart,
And make the Picture of my Love by Art:
For thou the first was he that did invent
To Figure Passions, and them to present
To object's sence; and if so, then I
May my Idea by my eyes descrie;
For all Ideas they, as precious prove,
They are not Substance, but in Substance move.

[Enter **MODE** to **OBSERVER** and **SPEND-ALL**.

**OBSERVER**
Are the Ladies coming into the Presence?

**MODE**
No, they all keep their beds to enjoy their Lovers so, as they sleep to dream, and dream to be embraced.

**OBSERVER**
They shall not need to do that, for they may be embraced awake.

**MODE**
O fie! that is an old out-worn fashion, and is more proper for old Ladies, then young.

**OBSERVER**
Sure you mistake; for Dreams are more proper for old Ladies, and waking-embraces for young.

**MODE**
Nay, then you mistake, for young Ladies love Amorous Contemplations, otherwise they would not delight so much in Romances as they do; but old Ladies who have more experience, and so are wiser, love the fruition of Realities; which makes them love young Men, not in Dreams or Romances, but in Courts and Cities.

**SPEND-ALL**
If so, then young Men may despair of young Women, and old Women not be jealous of young Women; and if I were sure of that, I would presently clap up a Match with an old doting Lady that I am acquainted withal, who is as rich as old.

**MODE**
You had best make hast for fear you should have Rivals; for if all young Men despair, the old Women will be so Wooed, that the multiplicity and choice will make them as nice, coy and proud, as the most prime young Beauties.

**SPEND-ALL**
You say true, wherefore I will be beforehand, and go to her before she hears of this dreaming-fashion.

**CONVERSANT**
But how if this fashion should soon change to a quite opposite?

**SPEND-ALL**
Yes, there is the danger; therefore I will not go.

[Enter the young Princess Melancholy, and some Ladies, whereof one rubs her eyes, the other gapes, the third stretches her self; all passing over the Stage.

**OBSERVER**

Lord bless us! what a drowsie fashion the Ladies have got?

**CONVERSANT**
But to my view, they were not so drowsie but they did leer upon us.

**MODE**
That was to view if any of us was the Man they dream'd of.

**OBSERVER**
O Lord! if it be thy will, let me be the Man the Princess dreams of.

**SPEND-ALL**
And I desire I might be the Man they all did dream of; which if so, the Grand Signior would not be better served, then I should; nor more numerously, for I should have all the young Women in the Kingdom.

**MODE**
If you had, you could not Marry them all.

**SPEND-ALL**
No, but I could Manage them all.

**MODE**
They would rather Manage you.

**SPEND-ALL**
I should be well pleas'd to be Managed by a young Lady.

**MODE**
But not by so many young Ladies as are in the Kingdom.

**OBSERVER**
If he were, he would be Managed so, as to be a lame Jade.

[Exeunt.


SCENE V

[Enter **LADY QUICK-WIT**, and **LADY SELF-CONCEIT**.

**LADY QUICK-WIT**
Self-conceit, the new Maids are come that are to be our Chamber-fellows.

**LADY SELF-CONCEIT**
Where, where are they? for God's sake, tell me quickly, I long to see them; but are they handsome?

**LADY QUICK-WIT**

No, by my troth; for one of them is so bashful, that what Beauty Nature hath given her, is spoiled for want of breeding; the other is none of Nature's choicest Pieces.

**LADY SELF-CONCEIT**
But what are they?

**LADY QUICK-WIT**
They are gone by the back-staires, to the Princess.

**LADY SELF-CONCEIT**
The Princess keeps her Chamber to day.

**LADY QUICK-WIT**
Yes, but she has permitted them into her Presence.

[Enter all the **GENTLEMEN**.

**LADY SELF-CONCEIT**
Gallants, are the new Maids come from the Princess?

**MODE**
No, we come to see them; for it is said, they are very handsome.

**LADY SELF-CONCEIT**
I have heard by two or three,
That they are not handsome.

**LADY QUICK-WIT**
They are coming, they are coming.

[Enter the **MOTHER**, and the **LADY BASHFUL**.

**MOTHER**
Where is the Princess, Gentlemen, to give the Oath to this young Lady?

[All the **GENTLEMEN** come to Salute Her.

**OBSERVER**
Mother, will you give me leave to Salute your
Daughter?

**MOTHER**
Should I not give you leave, you would take leave.

[He Salutes the **YOUNG MAID**.

**OBSERVER**
Lady, you will add to the Splendour of the Court.

**CONVERSANT**
Lady, you will advance the Glory of your
Sex.

[He Salutes Her.

**MODE**
Mother, you are one of the fortunatest Mothers that ever came to the Court; for here was never such a company of Beauties at one time, as is at this time.

**MOTHER**
Come, come, you are all Flatterers; wherefore my Daughter beware of them.

**LADY SELF-CONCEIT**
Mother, your new-come Daughter is bashful.

**LADY QUICK-WIT**
You must perswade her to hold up her head.

**LADY SELF-CONCEIT**
What eyes has she, black or gray?

**MOTHER**
Well, well, pray have patience; for by that time she has been in the Court so long as either of you, has been, she will be as confident as any in the Court.

**LADY QUICK-WIT**
But Mother where is your other new Danghter?

**MOTHER**
She is coming forth; and by my faith she is a metled Lass indeed. But come Daughter Bashful, we must go seek the Gentleman that must give you your Oath.

[Exit **MOTHER**, and **LADY BASHFUL**.

**LADY QUICK-WIT**
Lord! how simply she looks!

**MODE**
Give me a simple Girl; I love to teach, not to learn.

**LADY SELF-CONCEIT**
What a dull eye she has!

**CONVERSANT**
A Melancholy eye, for variety, sometimes pleases best.

**LADY SELF-CONCEIT**
She has an unfortunate brow.

**OBSERVER**
Her brows seem like a bow, that's ready bent to shoot Love's glances forth.

**LADY QUICK-WIT**
She hangs down her head as if she were working of Cross-stitch.

**SPEND-ALL**
She looks as if she would be as constant as Penelope was.

[Enter the other new **MAID**, the **LADY WAGTAIL**.

**LADY WAGTAIL**
Where is the Mother, is she always so confident of her Daughters, as to leave them to themselves?

**MODE**
I marry Sir, this Lady seems to have mettal.

**CONVERSANT**
She seems of a free Spirit.

**OBSERVER**
A Lady of an excellent Presence.

**SPEND-ALL**
There is life in her Countenance.

**LADY WAGTAIL**
Pray, Gentlemen, which way went the Mother?

[All the **GENTLEMEN** run out to seek the **MOTHER**, then return back and speak to Her.

**GENTLEMEN**
The Mother will come presently.

**LADY WAGTAIL**
Pray, Gentlemen, excuse me for troubling you; I should not have been so rude, but that I am ignorant of the wayes in Court, but I shall be industrious to learn them, and then I shall be ready to serve you.

**GENTLEMAN**
We are all your Vassals, Lady

[**LADY WAGTAIL** addresses her self to **LADY SELF-CONCEIT** and **QUICK-WIT**.

**LADY WAGTAIL**

Ladies, I shall be glad to have the honour of your Friendship, and to be endeared to such honourable Sisters.

**LADY SELF-CONCEIT**
We shall be ready to serve you.

[Enter **MRS WANTON**, one of the Maids of Honour, as running into the Room.

**MRS WANTON**
Where is my Comrade? where is my Comrade?

[**LADY WAGTAIL** and **MRS WANTON** meet, Embrace and Kiss each other.

**MRS WANTON**
Dear Wagtail, thou art according to my heart.

**LADY WAGTAIL**
My dear Wanton, I make no doubt, but we shall agree very well.

**MRS WANTON**
I was so joy'd, when I heard you were allotted to be my Chamber-fellow, for I was so afraid of that clod of dull Earth, the new come fellow; for it is reported that she makes Conditions not to be with such a Chamber-fellow that sits up late, or hath much Company.

**LADY WAGTAIL**
The Princess says, she must be in the Chamber of Mrs. Quick-wit.

**LADY QUICK-WIT**
She shall not lie with me, let her lie in the
Chamber of Mrs. Self-conceit.

**LADY SELF-CONCEIT**
With me? By my troth, that shall not be, for shall I that have been here this dozen years, have the rubbish thrown into my Chamber?

**MRS WANTON**
Why, then she must lie with the old Mother, there is no other place.

**LADY QUICK-WIT**
Why, the old Mother sits up as late with the old Signiors of the Court, as any of her Daughters do with the young Monsieurs.

[Exeunt **LADIES**.

**OBSERVER**
I hope if there be no room for the young Lady amongst Women, she will be forced to come to us Men for a Lodging.

**MODE**

Faith, we shall quarrel as much, who shall have her, as the Women do, to cast her out of their Company.

**SPEND-ALL**

I am of the Ladies mind, I would not willingly have her; for she appears with such a divine Purity, as if she would be apt to convert me from my Debauchery, and trouble my Conscience with Repentance.

[Exeunt.


SCENE VI

[Enter **QUICK-WIT** and **LADY WAGTAIL**.

**LADY QUICK-WIT**

Lady, I hear you have an admiring Servant.

**LADY WAGTAIL**

For God's sake Lady Quick-wit, tell me who it is?

**LADY QUICK-WIT**

You know who it is.

**LADY WAGTAIL**

Nay, prithee tell me; in faith I know not who it is.

**LADY QUICK-WIT**

You dissemble in making your self ignorant.

**LADY WAGTAIL**

In truth I do not know; wherefore prithee tell me, for I long to know who it is.

**LADY QUICK-WIT**

I hope your Servant has not put you into a longing humour?

**LADY WAGTAIL**

No, but you have, and therefore tell me.

**LADY QUICK-WIT**

'Tis reported, Monsieur Ape is your admiring Servant.

**LADY WAGTAIL**

Truly Monsieur Ape is a very fine Person.

**LADY QUICK-WIT**

Indeed he wears fine Clothes.

**LADY WAGTAIL**
The truth is, he is a neat spruce Courtier.

**LADY QUICK-WIT**
He ought to be so, spending most of his time in dressing and trimming himself.

**LADY WAGTAIL**
He is a very Civil Man to our Sex.

**LADY QUICK-WIT**
He is so, if it be a Civility to kiss the Ladies
Busks, Fans, Gloves, and the tails of their Gowns.

**LADY WAGTAIL**
He is a well-bred Gentleman.

**LADY QUICK-WIT**
Yes, if good breeding lies in the Heels, for he dances well.

**LADY WAGTAIL**
He is an exact Courtier.

**LADY QUICK-WIT**
'Tis true, for he Flatters and Complements.

**LADY WAGTAIL**
He is a great Scholar.

**LADY QUICK-WIT**
He is well read in Fashions, and studies new
Modes.

**LADY WAGTAIL**
He hath an Elegant speech.

**LADY QUICK-WIT**
And speaks in a Romancical stile.

**LADY WAGTAIL**
And he has a ready Wit.

**LADY QUICK-WIT**
To imitate Extravagancies.

**LADY WAGTAIL**
He is a Valiant Man.

**LADY QUICK-WIT**
To take foolish Women Prisoners.

**LADY WAGTAIL**
He is a Politick Man.

**LADY QUICK-WIT**
He is so, in pretending to have more power with the Emperor then he hath; by which means he gets Clients to Fee him, and simple ignorant Men to Bribe him, for which Fees and Bribes, they have fair words and large promises, but not any performances.

**LADY WAGTAIL**
I perceive Monsieur Ape is not your admiring
Servant, you speak so spitefully of him.

**LADY QUICK-WIT**
It seems I am not his admirer, I speak so truly of him.

**LADY WAGTAIL**
I must not hear any evil against my Servant
Monsieur Ape.

**LADY QUICK-WIT**
Then you must not hear him mentioned.

[Enter **LADY SELF-CONCEIT**, with her Portrait.

**LADY SELF-CONCEIT**
Quick-wit, I have been seeking you to shew you my Portrait.

**LADY QUICK-WIT**
What Painter drew it?

**LADY SELF-CONCEIT**
A Painter did not draw it, but a Poetical Lord did write it.

**LADY QUICK-WIT**
So I perceive a Portrait is a Mode-Phrase for a Character, or a Description; and a Portrait, Character and Description of Particulars, signifies one and the same thing.

**LADY SELF-CONCEIT**
Yes, but Characters and Descriptions have been so often used, writ and named, that the Readers are so weary'd with those old fashioned names, as it keeps them all from reading the matter or subject of such Writings.

**LADY QUICK-WIT**
So, then the word Portrait is to invite the Readers to read it.

**LADY SELF-CONCEIT**

No doubt of that, and well, if the word Portrait will perswade them to read it; but shall I read my Portrait to you?

**LADY QUICK-WIT**

Yes, I desire to hear a Portrait, for though I have seen many Portraits, yet I have never heard them speak.

**LADY SELF-CONCEIT** [Reads her Portrait]

Your Curls of Hair like Clouds, yet black as night;
Your Eyes as Stars do give a Sparkling light;
Your Forehead like the Heavens milky way;
Your Nose a hill of Snow in Valley lay;
Your Lips like Rosie-morn when th' Sun doth rise,
Shine on your Chin, as bright as he i'th' skies;
From whence the Beams dilated on your breast,
Do make a Torrid Zone 'tween East and West;
And those that do this Heav'nly Picture view,
Must needs confess 'twas only made for you.

**LADY QUICK-WIT**

Faith, this is like the Painter that drew a Rose for a Woodcock.

**LADY SELF-CONCEIT**

What, do you call me a Woodcock?

**LADY QUICK-WIT**

Why? a Woodcock is a fine Bird, and good Meat; but why did not this Portrait-maker draw or describe you no farther then the breast?

**LADY SELF-CONCEIT**

By reason many Persons Pictures are drawn no farther.

**LADY QUICK-WIT**

It was a shrewd sign, he could similize no farther.

**LADY SELF-CONCEIT**

He could not go beyond the Heavens.

**LADY QUICK-WIT**

In my opinion he has gone too great a Journey in going so far; for I believe it has made his Poetical feet, which I perceive to be diseased with the Gout, too weary; for he has travel'd through the Ecliptick line; but if he have crost the line, I think he must have gone from South to North, a very cold Climate.

**LADY SELF-CONCEIT**

I perceive you are spiteful at my Portrait, because you have not one made of you.

**LADY QUICK-WIT**

Can you blame me if I be spiteful to see you
Metamorphosed from a Terrestrial Body, to a Coelestial
Portrait.

[Enter **OBSERVER** and **CONVERSANT**.

**OBSERVER**
Ladies, how doth the Princess?

**LADY QUICK-WIT**
The Princess is very Melancholy, and it is fear'd she will fall into a Consumption.

**LADY SELF-CONCEIT**
But the Emperor to prevent it, will send for all the Gentry and Nobility in the Empire to present
themselves to the Princess, and whomsoever she likes, she shall have.

**CONVERSANT**
But how if her Idea should prove a Married Man?

**LADY QUICK-WIT**
The truth is, it disturbs the Thoughts of Married Wives; for those that love their Husbands, are afraid,
and those that care not for their Husbands hope; but all the Men are well pleased in hope of being
Emperor, for you know the Princess is Heir to the Crown.

[Enter **MODE**.

**MODE**
Lady, how doth the Princess?

**LADY QUICK-WIT**
She is as all Lovers are, Melancholy.

**MODE**
Are all Lovers Melancholy?

**LADY QUICK-WIT**
Yes, when they cannot enjoy their Beloved; and her Beloved is but a shadow, which the more it is
follow'd, the farther it flies; wherefore she is Melancholy, as being despised.

[**LADY** Self-conceit sighs.

**LADY QUICK-WIT**
What makes you sigh?

**LADY SELF-CONCEIT**
Faith, because I am not a Princess, to have my choice of all the Men in the Empire.

**LADY QUICK-WIT**

I would not be a Princess upon that condition, for I should be as much troubled to chuse, as to refuse.

**LADY SELF-CONCEIT**
That is a sign you love Men well.

**LADY QUICK-WIT**
Why say you so?

**LADY SELF-CONCEIT**
Because you express your trouble, that you should desire more then one, and be loth to deny any.

[Enter a **FOOL**.

**FOOL**
Oh Ladies, Oh the strange sights that I have seen! the monstrous strange sights that I have seen!

**LADY QUICK-WIT**
What monstrous sights have you seen?

**FOOL**
Why, I have seen strange Monsters!

**LADY QUICK-WIT**
What Monsters?

**FOOL**
I saw Men with strange Heads, and as strange Bodies; for they had the speech of Men, and the upright shape of Men, and yet were partly like as other Creatures; for one Man had an Asses head, and his body was like a Goose; another Man had a Jack-a-napes-head, but all his body was like a Baboon, and he shew'd tricks, as Jack-a-napes and Baboons use to do; another Man had a Swines head, and all his body was like a Goat; Another had a head like a Stag, with a large pair of branched Horns, and all his body was featur'd like a Woodcock, and his arms were feather'd as a Woodcocks wings, but he could not fly from his disgrace, for his Horned head did hinder the flight of his Wings; Then I saw a Woman that was not like a Mare-Maid, for Mare-Maids are like Women from the head to the waste, and from the waste like a Fish; but this Woman was like a Fish from the head to the waste, and from the waste like a Beast; so that she was a Batons rompus; Another Woman had the eyes of a Crocodile, but her body was like a changeable Cameleon; and many other Monstrous Creatures did I see.

**LADY SELF-CONCEIT**
Where did you see those Monsters?

**FOOL**
Where they are to be seen.

**LADY SELF-CONCEIT**
Where is that?

**FOOL**

In Dreams, when I was asleep.

**LADY QUICK-WIT**
It seems you have a Fool's head that dreams such fantastical Dreams.

**FOOL**
The wisest and gravest heads that are, do dream such Dreams; for a Philosopher's head hath butter-flies Dreams; and a Politician, although he has a Foxes head when he is awake, yet he has but an Asse's head when he sleeps.

**LADY QUICK-WIT**
You are a Knave awake, and a Fool asleep.

**FOOL**
Then I am a wise Man.

**LADY QUICK-WIT**
Is a Knave a wise Man?

**FOOL**
According to the foolishness of the World he is; for if the World of Mankind, which is the most part, were not Fools. Knaves could not cozen them; and those are wiser that deceive, then those that are deceived; at least, they are accounted so by those Fools they have deceived.

**LADY SELF-CONCEIT**
You speak like an Ass.

**FOOL**
If I speak like Balaam 's Ass, I speak wisely; but truly Ladies I had a pleasant Dream.

**LADY QUICK-WIT**
What Dream was that?

**FOOL**
I dream'd that all the Princess Maids of Honour did dance about me, and after that they did all kiss me, which was very pleasant to me; for though they danced like Apes, they kissed like Courtisans.

**LADY QUICK-WIT**
Out, you Rogue, do you say we kiss like
Courtisans.

**FOOL**
Why all Women kiss alike, ask the Gentlemen.

[Exit **FOOL**.

**LADY SELF-CONCEIT**
Come Quick-wit, let us go and see how the

Princess doth.

[Exeunt.

**OBSERVER**
The Ladies are much concerned for the Princess
Sickness.

**MODE**
I believe they are all troubled with that Disease, although they are more crafty to conceal it.

**CONVERSANT**
The Emperor is very strict to the Princess, sothat he will not suffer any Man to come near her but
Mimick the fool; and he is only suffered to divert her Melancholy.

**OBSERVER**
He is more a Knave then a Fool; wherefore he might more safely have trusted the wisest Man in the
Kingdom.


SCENE VII

[The **PRINCESS** lies upon a Couch as sick, and her eyes shut. Soft Musick is heard, and a Song sung.

**FOOL** [Singing, off-stage]
You God of Sleep send Dreams for to restore
The Princess mind to be as 'twas before;
Or else you other Gods that dwell above,
Cause her to dream of a Seraphick Love:
Let not her Mortal Soul so cloud the Light
Of her Immortal Soul that shines so bright.
Cast out the vain Idea from her brain,
That nothing of that Figure may remain.

[After this, the **FOOL**: standing at the Door, sings a part of an Old Ballet; as follows.

This long seven years and more, have I still lov'd thee,
Do then my joy restore, fair Lady pity me,
Pity my grievous pains long suffer'd for thy sake,
Which will not let me rest, for no rest can I take:
Fair Lady pity me, do not my Suit deny,
O yield me some relief that shall for sorrow die.
How can I pity thee, the Lady then repli'd,
I am no Match for thee, thy Suit must be deny'd;
I am of Royal blood, thou of a mean degree,
It stands not for my Good that I should Marry thee:
This Answer oft I had, which struck my heart full deep,

And on my bed full soft did I lie down and weep.

[Singing the last Verse, the **FOOL** enters, and the **PRINCESS** awakes.

**PRINCESS**
How dare you disturb me with your Foolery?

**FOOL**
Fools never disturb, for we are made for Laughter, not for anger.

**PRINCESS**
Carry away the Fool to the Porters Lodge, and let him be soundly whipt.

**FOOL**
No, carry the Princess to the Emperors Chamber, and let her there be whipt, for she is more Fool then I; for she is in love with a Dream, and I am in love with a Princess; the truth is, I have a great desire to be an Emperor, and you had better love a Fool then a Shadow.

**PRINCESS**
In truth I will tell the Emperor my Father.

**FOOL**
I faith, that will not help you; for he is wise, and knows I am the fittest Match for you; for he knows that when two Fools Marry, they make but one Fool; and he will chuse rather to have but one Fool then two; and when we are Married we shall make one grand Fool, and that will amount, and be as much as indifferently wise.

**PRINCESS**
I will have your Tongue cut out of your
Head.

**FOOL**
You will as soon cut off my Head; but let me tell you, You shall not; nay by'r Lady, you must not be in this humour, the Emperor commands it, as also that you shall come to him.

[Exeunt **OMNES**.

ACT II

SCENE I

[Enter **SPEND-ALL** in a fine Suit of Clothes, meeting **CONVERSANT**.

**CONVERSANT**
Jupiter bless us! how fine and brave you are, in a rich
Suit of Clothes; is this your Wedding day?

**SPEND-ALL**

No, this day is not my Wedding day; but this Suit is my Wooing-Suit, for I am going to Woo an old Lady, who is very Rich.

**CONVERSANT**

Is she Wise?

**SPEND-ALL**

I hope not, for if she were, she would never grant my Suit; but if she be a Fool, as I hope she is, then Youth and Bravery will win her.

**CONVERSANT**

And the more sprightly, lively, and fantastical you appear, the better the old Lady will like you.

**SPEND-ALL**

I believe you; but I doubt that the sight of the old Lady will put me into so dull and Melancholy a humour, as I shall not please her.

**CONVERSANT**

Imagine her a young Beauty.

**SPEND-ALL**

I cannot imagine her a young Beauty, when I see her; for Imagination works only upon absent Objects.

**CONVERSANT**

Then think her your Reverend Grand-Dame.

**SPEND-ALL**

That will make me think of death, she being dead.

**CONVERSANT**

Nay faith, she will rather make you think of a
Resurrection.

**SPEND-ALL**

Can I think an old wrinkled Woman, a glorified body?

**CONVERSANT**

I forgot the Glory, I only thought of
Life; but however, you may think her a Saint.

**SPEND-ALL**

That I cannot, if she marry me, a young, vain, deboist Man, which is, a Sinner.

**CONVERSANT**

Imagine she Marries you to convert you from
Evil to Good.

**SPEND-ALL**

Nay faith, she would sooner pervert me, were I good, to evil; but were she a wise, reverend, virtuous aged Woman, I could love her better then a wanton young Filly; also, I should be ruled and govern'd by her experienced advice and counsel; but those ancient Women that are so, will not Marry a wild, vain young Man.

**CONVERSANT**

There is not any thing that can rule, advise, or govern you, but Time.

**SPEND-ALL**

Why, an ancient Woman is Time; for though she be not old Father Time, yet she is old Mother Time.

**CONVERSANT**

Well, go to the old Lady, woo her, win her, and Marry her; for if you will wink, or shut your eyes, she will be as pleasing as a young Wife.

**SPEND-ALL**

Would you have me a blind Wooer, and a blind Husband?

**CONVERSANT**

It would be happy for some Husbands if they were blind, that they might not see their own disgrace; for many a Husband sees his Neighbour in bed with his Wife; and it would be great wisdom in old Women, if they would, or must of necessity, Marry a young Man, to Marry a blind young Man, that he might not see her decays, ruines and wrinkles.

**SPEND-ALL**

Well, I will go and try if I can perswade this old Lady to Marry me.

**CONVERSANT**

Do so, for it may become a fashion for young
Men to Marry old Women.

[Enter **LADY BASHFUL**, **SPEND-ALL** addresses himself to her.

**SPEND-ALL**

Lady, I was a while since in the Privy Chamber, where my eyes did search for you, but they could not single you out from the rest of the Ladies.

**LADY BASHFUL**

It seems that either you were blind, or that I had not any Beauty.

**SPEND-ALL**

The Ladies in Court, when they stand close together, are like the Heaven's milky way; for the number of Stars appears like a thick white stream, so as no particular Star can be discerned.

**LADY BASHFUL**

I had rather be a Meteor singly alone, then a

Star in a Crowd.

[Exit.

[Enter **LADY QUICK-WIT**.

**SPEND-ALL**
Lady, will you give me leave to be your admiring Servant?

**LADY QUICK-WIT**
The truth is, we Ladies in Court have so many Courting-Servants, that we know not how to govern them.

**SPEND-ALL**
I shall be govern'd easily; for I will watch your looks with admiration, listen to your words with great attention, study your thoughts with serious Contemplation, and obey all your Commands with pious devotion.

**LADY QUICK-WIT**
Admiration dazles the sight, sight stops the hearing, hearing hinders the thinking, and action is an enemy to study.

**SPEND-ALL**
You have so much Wit, Lady, that your Wit is able to govern the whole World.

**LADY QUICK-WIT**
Wit can easier make a World, then govern a World; for Wit is a better architect then Governor; in truth Wit cannot rule it self; for Wit is ruled by Judgment; and thus by mispraising Wit, you have done Judgment wrong.

[Exit **QUICK-WIT**.

**SPEND-ALL**
Faith, I am an unfortunate Man in Courtships.

**CONVERSANT**
That is, because you Complement with the
Ladies, that love to have Men talk to them rudely.

**SPEND-ALL**
Well, I will try my own way of Courtship once more, if I can converse with any of them again.

**CONVERSANT**
Then you shall never win their favours.

[Enter **LADY SELF-CONCEIT**.

**SPEND-ALL**
Lady, you are finer drest then any Lady in the Court.

**LADY SELF-CONCEIT**

'Tis a sign I want Beauty, that I am forced to use the art of dressing; and you the flattery of Commendations, seeing I had not Beauty worthy of a true praise.

**SPEND-ALL**

The Court is the Sphere of Beauty, Lady.

**LADY SELF-CONCEIT**

And Men are Beauties Gazers.

**SPEND-ALL**

Men are Love's Astronomers, Lady.

**LADY SELF-CONCEIT**

And what new Star-like Beauty have you found out?

**SPEND-ALL**

You, Lady.

[Exit **LADY SELF-CONCEIT** without Answering.

**SPEND-ALL**

Oh happy Man that I am, for I am a Conqueror.

**CONVERSANT**

Of what are you a Conqueror, of Wit?

**SPEND-ALL**

No of Love; for silence gives consent.

**CONVERSANT**

But you did not woo her to love.

**SPEND-ALL**

Not woo her! prithee what have I been speaking all this while?

**CONVERSANT**

Why, you have been Complementing.

**SPEND-ALL**

'Tis true, and Complements are Lovers
Wooings.

**CONVERSANT**

But you forget the old Lady; you were going to woo before you saw these young Ladies.

**SPEND-ALL**

Hang Old Ladies, give me a Young Lady.

**CONVERSANT**
But consider, the old Lady is rich.

**SPEND-ALL**
'Tis true, and I want wealth; wherefore I'le go a wooing to the old Lady, and leave my heart with the young Ladies; but now I think better of it; I will not go, for I believe you stay here to watch a time, to get one of these young Beauties alone.

**CONVERSANT**
No, no, I will stay here to be an Agent in love, for you.

**SPEND-ALL**
I desire no such Agent as you; for you are a subtile, slie Gentleman; you will take your time and opportunity; besides, you have Lands and Money, which will winn a young Lady sooner, then fine Clothes and Complements will do.

**CONVERSANT**
Prithee be not jealous; for young Ladies are not so wise as to love prudently.

**SPEND-ALL**
What a Pox should you dwell in this
Room, if it were not for some such design?

**CONVERSANT**
I stay here to observe Humours, hear Wit, and to see Beauties.

**SPEND-ALL**
And not to make Love?

**CONVERSANT**
No.

**SPEND-ALL**
If it be so, then, prithee, praise me to the young Ladies.

**CONVERSANT**
I will, I will.

**SPEND-ALL**
Do not forget any of my good parts.

**CONVERSANT**
I cannot forget them; for I do not remember any you have.

[Exit **SPEND-ALL**

[Enter **OBSERVER**.

**CONVERSANT**
Observer, I wonder you will be absent out of this Room, in regard you only come to observe the Court beauties and Court-wits.

**OBSERVER**
Faith, I became tired and wearied of the observations in this Room, the Presence; and so I went into the Privy-Chamber to observe the Emperor.

**CONVERSANT**
And how did he appear?

**OBSERVER**
He did appear in Majesty, as far beyond his Royalty, as his Royalty appears above his meanest Subjects.

**CONVERSANT**
Then he appear'd as a God.

**OBSERVER**
Indeed he appear'd above what is mortal.

**CONVERSANT**
And did you hear him speak?

**OBSERVER**
Yes; and he was in so witty a vein, that my Hearing was (as if it were) tyed to his speech, and my Mind so fill'd with delight, that I had not power to stir from the place I stood, but both my body and mind were (as 'twere) fixt to a Deitical Centre.

**CONVERSANT**
I perceive, that you, instead of an Observer, are become a Courtier; and now you have learn'd to flatter.

**OBSERVER**
Not so, for by Heav'n I speak the truth of my thoughts and belief; for though I do not believe the Emperor to be a God, yet God and Nature have made, and endued him, to be above all other Men; for name me any other Prince or private Man in this age, that has that sweet Nature, excellent Qualities, experienced Knowledg, clear Understanding, upright Justice, Heroick Courage, free Generosity, and divine Clemency as he has; and if you match him in all the known World, proclaim me a Fool and a Lyar, which is to be a Flatterer, a Vice I hate.

**CONVERSANT**
I confess, there are two Reasons that perswade me to be of your mind; the first is, That I have observed the same in the Emperor; the second is, That I did never know you to flatter, dissemble, or speak false in my life; for you are so infinitely proud, that you will not descend so low as to flatter, or be so humble in praises, were it to God himself.

**OBSERVER**

God is too Omnipotent for Praise, and our Emperor too Heroick and truly Royal for Flattery; so that the one is not a subject for praise, nor the other for Flattery.

[Enter **LADY QUICK-WIT**, **LADY SELF-CONCEIT**, **MRS WANTON** and **LADY WAGTAIL**

**LADY SELF-CONCEIT**
I will tell you a Wonder.

**LADY QUICK-WIT**
What Wonder?

**LADY SELF-CONCEIT**
Why, I found Mrs. Bashful alone with a Man.

**LADY QUICK-WIT**
Why, that's no wonder to see a Man and a Woman alone, especially in the Court; for we watch all opportunities, upon every occasion, to be so.

**LADY SELF-CONCEIT**
But 'tis a wonder to see Bashful alone with a Man, and abroad too; for she shuns Men, as she would do Serpents, and locks her Chamber-doors against them, and accounts it a crime to be seen undress'd, and a sin not to be forgiven, to be seen in bed.

**LADY QUICK-WIT**
Why, she was neither in bed, nor undrest, I suppose.

**LADY SELF-CONCEIT**
No, she was at Madam Civilities house, and 'tis to be hoped she will come to it in time, when she has so much wit, as to hold a Discourse.

**MRS WANTON**
She hold a Discourse! she wants the Capacity, she wants the Capacity.

**LADY WAGTAIL**
Nay, you can give the best relation or description of her; for you were her bed-fellow.

**LADY SELF-CONCEIT**
Prithee what is she? a meer Mope; doth she never speak or discourse to you?

**MRS WANTON**
You shall judge, whether she doth or not; for she will never ask a question, nor make a doubt, nor give her opinion upon any thing.

[Enter **LADY BASHFUL**.

**LADY QUICK-WIT**
Come poor Bashful, there is none makes much of thee.

**LADY BASHFUL**
I should be loth to be made much of, after the
Court-fashion.

**LADY WAGTAIL**
After the Court-fashion! how is that? express it, express it.

**LADY BASHFUL**
Nay, you can express it best.

**LADY QUICK-WIT**
Faith, I pity thee for having no Servant.

**LADY BASHFUL**
I had rather be pitied for having no Servant, then censured for having too many.

**LADY SELF-CONCEIT**
If you be a good Girl, and do as the rest of your Honourable Sisters, or as all Court-Ladies do, I will send
you some of my worn Servants to Court you.

**LADY BASHFUL**
No, pray keep them as a store, lest you should want your self.

[Exit **LADY BASHFUL**

**LADY SELF-CONCEIT**
Faith, she is fitter for a Nunnery, then a
Court.

**LADY QUICK-WIT**
But I observe the Court has improved her
Wit.

**MRS WANTON**
Nay, the Court is the only Place to make
Fools, Wits.

**LADY QUICK-WIT**
Or Wits, Fools.

[Exeunt.

[Enter **SPEND-ALL**, and **CONVERSANT**

**CONVERSANT**
Monsieur Spend-All, how do you prosper in your old Lady's affection?

**SPEND-ALL**
Faith, more prosperously then I desire.

**CONVERSANT**
Would not you willingly enjoy her.

**SPEND-ALL**
Yes her Wealth, but not her Person.

**CONVERSANT**
You must take the worse with the better; for
I have observed, that Fortune, Fate, Nature, and the
Gods, mix Good and Evil, Pleasure and Discontent,
Health and Sickness together.

**SPEND-ALL**
I confess there is not any thing perfect, or pure in Nature; but God be praised in his Creatures, and all things.

**CONVERSANT**
Then God be praised for the love of the old
Lady to you.

**SPEND-ALL**
I have much strife with my self to give praises for her; but I desire and should give thanks to see some of the young Ladies, that I might converse with them to revive me from death to life, from hate to love.

[Enter **LADY QUICK-WIT**

**SPEND-ALL**
Lady, you are the life of the Court.

**LADY QUICK-WIT**
And the Court is the life of me, Sir.

**SPEND-ALL**
Your Eyes give light to all the beholders.

**LADY QUICK-WIT**
I had rather my wit could give life to all the
Hearers.

**SPEND-ALL**
But your Beauty doth excell all the Beauties in the Court.

**LADY QUICK-WIT**
Until you converse with another Lady, and then her Beauty doth as far excell mine, as mine at this present doth excell others.

**SPEND-ALL**
Indeed, Beauty appears best in Conversation.

**LADY QUICK-WIT**
And worse with often viewing.

**SPEND-ALL**
No more then the light of the Sun doth.

**LADY QUICK-WIT**
The more the Sun is gaz'd upon, the blinder the sight is.

**SPEND-ALL**
That is the reason the splendor of the Sun's light doth over-power the sight.

**LADY QUICK-WIT**
Why, then the splendor puts out the sight of his light, which buries his glory in the darkness of blindness; and if my Beauty doth the like, I am sorry for it; for I would not have such a Beauty as digs its own grave in the Eyes of its admirers; but as a moderate Light, so moderate a Beauty pleases the sight best.

[Exit **LADY QUICK-WIT**

[Enter **LADY SELF-CONCEIT**

**SPEND-ALL**
Lady, there is not any Man doth more admire you, then I.

**LADY SELF-CONCEIT**
If I have Merit, you ought to give Merit its due; and if I am worthy of admiration, I am bound to the Gods and Nature for their favours, and not to you for your Praises.

**SPEND-ALL**
But all men do neither honour, nor admire what is worthy of either.

**LADY SELF-CONCEIT**
If they do not, the injury is to Nature and the Gods.

[Exit **LADY SELF-CONCEIT**

**CONVERSANT**

Faith, Spend-all, your Complements will not serve you in Love-matters.

**SPEND-ALL**
I confess they are not fortunate.

[Enter **LADY BASHFUL**

**SPEND-ALL**
Madam, I wonder you should hide any part of your Face with Black-patches, your Face being fair and lovely.

**LADY BASHFUL**
Black-patches curiously cut and stuck upon the Face, are like wise Sentences in a Speech, they give Grace and Lustre.

[Enter **LADY SELF-CONCEIT**

**LADY SELF-CONCEIT**
Lady Bashful, I have been seeking you all the Court over, in every Lodging, and I could not find you.

**LADY BASHFUL**
You see, I am not lost, for here I am; but where's the Lady Quickwit ?

**LADY SELF-CONCEIT**
She is within, and asks for you.

[Enter **QUICK-WIT**.

**LADY QUICK-WIT**
O! it is so cold! so very cold, as it is able to freeze all the Lovers hearts in the Court and City!

**CONVERSANT**
And not in the Country, Lady?

**LADY QUICK-WIT**
O no, for those that dwell in the Country, make such great Blazing-fires, as they thaw Cold, and heat Love.

**CONVERSANT**
Love doth not require Heat, for it is sufficiently hot of it self.

**LADY QUICK-WIT**
Yes, when it is in a Fever, in which Love most commonly dies: But come Ladies, shall we go to Supper?

**SPEND-ALL**
Conversant, tell Lady Quick-wit, I am in Love with her.

**CONVERSANT**

Lady, Monsieur Spend-all sayes, he is in Love with you.

**LADY QUICK-WIT**

I hate to hear of Love by a Second, it seems so like a Challenge.

[Exeunt all the **LADIES**.

**SPEND-ALL**

Faith, Court-Ladies have quick Wits.

**CONVERSANT**

They are bred to answer, they are so often spoke to, but of all the Ladies, I confess, I like the Lady Quick-wit.

**SPEND-ALL**

Faith, I like them all so well, I know not which to like best; and I wish with all my heart, they all would like me as well as my old Lady doth; Oh, what a happy Man should I be, for I should have variety of Pleasures!

[Exeunt.

SCENE IV

[Enter **WAGTAIL**, and **MRS WANTON**.

**MRS WANTON**

The Lord of Loyalty sent me a merry Letter to day; and in the Letter, a Copy of Verses, desiring me to give them to Madam Bashful.

**LADY WAGTAIL**

Faith, those Verses will make her so conceited with her self, that she will be so proud, as to think her self the only she in the Court; wherefore, let me advise you not to give them her.

**MRS WANTON**

But what shall I say to the Lord of Loyalty, if he should ask me, whether I had given them to her.

**LADY WAGTAIL**

Put it off with Rallery.

[Enter the **MOTHER**, and **OBSERVER**

**MRS WANTON**

Mother, where is your Daughter Bashful, she is not here to attend the Princess coming forth?

**MOTHER**

She is gone abroad.

**LADY WAGTAIL**
Yes, to meet the Lord Loyalty.

**MRS WANTON**
Indeed Mother, you are too blame, to let your Daughters go abroad without you; and if the Princess should know of it, she would be very angry.

**MOTHER**
Why, she ask'd the Princess leave.

**LADY WAGTAIL**
It is a shame she should be abroad without the Mother; it is enough to disgrace all the Sister-hood; and therefore for Juno 's sake, send for her home.

**OBSERVER**
Why Ladies, I have known the Princess's Maids many times to go abroad without the Mother, and no disgrace to their Honour.

**MRS WANTON**
But not to meet such Company as she is gone to, for all the Kingdom knows, the Lord of Loyalty is none of the chastest men; and he courts her for her Youth and Beauty; 'tis not likely he will marry her; for he loves Variety too well, to tie himself to one.

**OBSERVER**
Truly I am of that opinion; but she is so Vertuous, she cannot be corrupted.

[Enter **LADY SELF-CONCEIT**.

**LADY SELF-CONCEIT**
Mother, the Princess is very angry that Madamoisel Bashful is gone abroad without you; she says, that though she gave her leave to go abroad, she thought she had so much discretion as to take the Mother along with her; but you must send for her presently.

**MRS WANTON**
Go, go, quickly Mother, quickly.

**LADY WAGTAIL**
I will go for her.

**MRS WANTON**
Nay, I will go for her.

**LADY SELF-CONCEIT**
Nay, pray stay, and let the Mother go her self.

[Enter **OBSERVER**, **CONVERSANT**.

**CONVERSANT**
Monsieur Observer, I heard a Lady say, you were a Fool.

**OBSERVER**
Ladies may say what they please.

**CONVERSANT**
But it seems, you have not pleased her, that she calls you Fool.

**OBSERVER**
It seems I have not courted her.

**CONVERSANT**
Are Ladies never pleas'd but when they are
Courted?

**OBSERVER**
No Faith; for then they think they are not thought Handsom.

**CONVERSANT**
Indeed Women delight in their Beauties.

**OBSERVER**
Not unless men admire their Beauties; for they are delighted with their Beauties, for the delight of Courtship; Beauty gets them Suiters; for were they ill-favoured, they would never be wooed.

**CONVERSANT**
But when they are wooed, they are not presently wonne.

**OBSERVER**
Yes Faith, they are wonne before they be wooed; and being wooed, they presently yield.

**CONVERSANT**
The truth is, Women have kind natures.

**OBSERVER**
Not so kind as willing.

**CONVERSANT**
Women are Loving-creatures.

**OBSERVER**
Yes, they are Self-lovers.

**CONVERSANT**
Not when they give themselves to men.

**OBSERVER**
They give themselves to men, because men should give themselves to them.

**CONVERSANT**
So they love men out of self-interest.

**OBSERVER**
No doubt of it.

**CONVERSANT**
You are an unjust Man.

**OBSERVER**
In what?

**CONVERSANT**
In dispraising all the Sex out of a displeasure to one Woman, for calling you Fool.

**OBSERVER**
I should not only be call'd a fool, but should prove my self one, if I should regard what Women say.

[Enter **MONSIEUR WEDLOCK**

**CONVERSANT**
Monsieur Wedlock, how doth your Lady?

**WEDLOCK**
She is groaning and complaining.

**CONVERSANT**
What is she in labour?

**WEDLOCK**
No, but she is breeding.

**CONVERSANT**
Monsieur Spend-all, I hear you are entring into the Matrimonial Order.

**SPEND-ALL**
Yes, Faith, I am going into the Order of
Cuckolds, Wittals, or Fools.

**OBSERVER**
Why, Marriage is an honourable Order.

**SPEND-ALL**
The Order is as it proves; but if you think it so honourable, why will not you be one of this Matrimonial Order?

**OBSERVER**
Because I am not ambitious of such Honours; but is the Lady you are to Marry very beautiful, Monsieur Spend-all?

**SPEND-ALL**
No, but she is Rich.

**WEDLOCK**
Is she of honourable birth?

**SPEND-ALL**
No, but she is Rich.

**WEDLOCK**
Is she well bred?

**SPEND-ALL**
No, but she is Rich.

**WEDLOCK**
Is she wise?

**SPEND-ALL**
No, but she is Rich.

**WEDLOCK**
Do you Marry only for Riches?

**SPEND-ALL**
Yes; for Necessity forces me to Marry an ill-favoured, foolish, old doting Woman.

**WEDLOCK**
Much good may she do you.

**SPEND-ALL**
Nay faith, she will not do me any good, unless she would die soon; but her Wealth will do me much good, and I shall prove an excellent Husband to her Riches.

**OBSERVER**
You are so deboist and wild, that you cannot be a good Husband to any thing.

**SPEND-ALL**

But I shall; for when I am so rich, as to have wherewithal to spend, I shall then be so thrifty as to spare; for it is to be observed, That Rich Men for the most part are miserable and covetous, when those that have but little, spend all they have, or can get.

**OBSERVER**
Pray bring me to visit this old foolish Lady you are to Marry.

**SPEND-ALL**
You must pardon me; if she were wise and young, I would let you see her; but being old and foolish, I dare not, lest you should entice her from me; for Old Women are more unconstant then Young; and being foolish, she will be so various, that her mind may change like the wind.

**OBSERVER**
You may trust me, were she young, beautiful, chast, honourable, well-bred, witty and rich; for I will never Marry.

**SPEND-ALL**
Yes, if you could get a Wife, with all these
Excellencies.

**OBSERVER**
I would not Marry, could I get a Wife with all those fore-mentioned Excellencies, as you call them; for were she young, she would want discretion, for want of Experience; were she beautiful, she would make me jealous, for Beauty is Courted; were she honoured with title, she would strive to rule, and would not be ruled; were she that which is named good breeding, which is to Fiddle, Dance, Sing, and speak divers Languages, and to know the Female and Masculine Genders in Languages, she would Gossip abroad, and seek out Company, and be at all Publick Meetings, to shew her breeding; if she have Wit, she will be always talking, and always opposing, to prove her Wit; if she be chast, she will be proud; if she be fruitful, she will be sickly and froward; if she be rich, she will spend much, because she brought much, and in the end will make me poorer then I am; and on the other side, were she old, I should not imbrace her; were she ill-favoured, I should have an aversion against her; were she of mean birth, and ill breeding, I should be asham'd of her; were she a fool, I should not regard her; were she poor, I should despise her; were she false, I should part from her.

**SPEND-ALL**
Well, Monsieur Observer, since you will neither Marry old, nor young, handsome, nor ill-favoured, chast nor wanton, mean nor honourable, foolish nor wise, poor nor rich, but are resolved to live a Batchellor, I will bring you to be acquainted with my old Mistress, that must be my old Wife, and Mr. Wedlock will bring you acquainted with his young Wife.

**WEDLOCK**
By my faith, but I will not.

**SPEND-ALL**
No, why?

**WEDLOCK**

Because he doth not declare he will not make Courtships to Wives, though he declares he will not have a Wife; and unless he declare and profess, he will not make love to other Men's Wives, I will not bring him acquainted with my Wife.

**SPEND-ALL**
Why, do you mistrust your Wife?

**WEDLOCK**
No, but I mistrust him; and were I sure my Wife would not yield, yet I do not love she should be tempted: But howsoever, to keep a Wife safe, is, to keep her close from Courtships, and from Masculine Acquaintance.

**CONVERSANT**
But Women will get liberty one way or other, if they have a wanton mind, and desire change.

**WEDLOCK**
Yet it is the part of a wise Husband to do his endeavour to keep her honest.

**OBSERVER**
 Well, I will neither visit Monsieur Spend-all 's old Mistress, nor your young  Wife; but I'le go with you to a merry Meeting, where I suppose, there will be those Women that will better please me, then the old Woman, and easier be enjoyed then your young Wife; wherefore, if you will go, Gentlemen, I will present you a Supper.

**SPEND-ALL**
If you will present us with Mistresses, we will go with you.

**OBSERVER**
They will present themselves.

[Enter **MONSIEUR MODE** to the rest.

**SPEND-ALL**
Monsieur Mode, it is reported, that you have the art to Court two or three Mistresses at one time; which if you have, I shall desire to be your Scholar, for I could never be in the favour of two Mistresses at one time; for the Courting of one lost me the other, and those I lose, become my Enemies.

**MODE**
He is a poor Man that hath but one Mistress; and he is a fool in Courtship, that cannot Court half a dozen Mistresses at one time.

**SPEND-ALL**
So, by this you call me a poor fool.

**MODE**
If you were not a fool, you would not desire to be my Scholar; and if you were not poor, you would not desire more then you have.

**SPEND-ALL**

Then make me wiser and richer.

**MODE**

Would you be wiser for profit, or wiser for pleasure.

**SPEND-ALL**

For pleasure!

**MODE**

Would you be richer for Wealth, or richer for Honour, or richer in a number of Mistresses?

**SPEND-ALL**

Richer in a number of Mistresses.

**MODE**

Then be bold, rude, and vain, talk much without sense, swear much without cause, brag much without reason, accoutre your self fantastically, behave your self carelesly, and imploy time idly; and be sure you raile of all Women generally, but praise every particular one, but so as in a general way, as some for one thing, and some for another, as you shall think best, by which you will keep them all in hopes; for if you should praise only one, that one will be too proud, and then disdain you, and the rest through dispair will hate you; also in your actions you must behave your self generally, as in a careless way, dividing your Courtships amongst them all, as to kiss one Woman's hand, another's neck, a third Woman's lips, embrace a fourth, rally with a fifth, and bed with the sixth; and after this manner you may Court twenty Mistresses at least at one time, and serve your self in private with them all one after another; for though you may Court many Mistresses at one time in publick, yet in private you must have but one at a time, and she will believe, or at least make her self believe, she is the only she that is beloved.

**SPEND-ALL**

I will follow your Instruction; and if I thrive,
I will give you thanks.

**MODE**

But if you be not ingenious, and well practised, my Instructions will do you but little good; for you may be like Players, that have excellent parts, and spoile them in the Acting; or like a Minister that chuses a good Text, and wants Oratory to preach of it; or you may be like a bungling Taylor that spoiles a fine Suit of Clothes with ill making: But if you will thrive, you must be of many Professions; and if you will be a Master of Courtship, you must be learned in the Liberal Arts and Sciences; you must be an Astrologer to foresee your Times, and their Times; an Astronomer to find out their Humours; a Cosmographer to measure their Capacities; a Philosopher, to pierce into their Natures and Dispositions; a Logician, to make their Vanities and Vices appear Vertues; an Arithmetician, to number their Praises, and cipher their Follies; and a Mathematician to draw them to your desires and delights.

**SPEND-ALL**

I shall do my best endeavour; but I fear that most Women are not worth so much pains, study and practice.

**MODE**

As for that, your idle Times must judg of it.

**SPEND-ALL**
Well, I will go to my Lodgings, and consider it.

**MODE**
Nay, faith, Consideration will spoile all my
Instructions.

[Exit **SPEND-ALL**, the **REST** stays.

[Enter **LADY WAGTAIL**, **MRS WANTON**, **LADY SELF-CONCEIT**, and **LADY BASHFUL**, as also the **MOTHER**.

**LADY SELF-CONCEIT**
'Tis well you are come, I would not be in your condition for any thing.

**LADY WAGTAIL**
I'faith, you will be talk'd withal.

**MRS WANTON**
If I were in so sad a condition, I know what I know.

**LADY BASHFUL**
Why Ladies, I have neither deserved Imprisonment, nor Death, which is the worst that can come unto me; but if I be condemned, I shall suffer both with patience and with courage.

**LADY SELF-CONCEIT**
O Lord! she speaks freely.

**LADY WAGTAIL**
She has found a Tongue since she went.

**LADY WAGTAIL**
'Tis well, if she has lost nothing, since she went.

**LADY SELF-CONCEIT**
On my word you have done very ill, which you deserve to be chid for.

**MRS WANTON**
I believe the Princess will turn you away.

**LADY BASHFUL**
I am very sorry I have offended the Princess; but yet I have done nothing but what I had her leave for.

[Enter **LADY QUICK-WIT**.

**LADY QUICK-WIT**
Madamoisel Bashful, you must come to the

Princess.

[Exeunt **LADY BASHFUL** and **LADY QUICK-WIT**.

**OBSERVER** [To the Moth]
Alas poor Mother we were all afraid you were kill'd.

**MOTHER**
Kill'd, who should kill me?

**OBSERVER**
Why, a rough, rude Coachman.

**MOTHER**
Which way should he kill me?

**OBSERVER**
With tumbling you over.

**MOTHER**
How tumbling me over?

**OBSERVER**
With your head downwards, and your heels upwards.

[Enter **LADY QUICK-WIT**.

**LADY SELF-CONCEIT**
What News? what News? what doth Madamoisel
Bashful confess?

**MRS WANTON**
What doth she confess?

**LADY QUICK-WIT**
Why, she confesses, she was at Madamoisel
Civilitie 's house, where she met the Lord Loyalty.

**LADY WAGTAIL**
And what said the Princess then?

**LADY QUICK-WIT**
Why the Princess chid her for offering to meet any Man without her leave; But she has pardon'd her for this time, and you must go all to the back-stairs, and stay there to wait on the Princess into the Gallery.

[Exeunt **WOMEN**.

**MODE**

I would the Ladies had as much love for me, as they are angry with their fellow-Lady.

**CONVERSANT**
If they had, they would overpower you with their kindness.

**MODE**
I would desire nothing more but to be so overpower'd.

[Enter **LADY SELF-CONCEIT** in hast running over the Stage.

**LADY SELF-CONCEIT**
Run, run.

[Enter **LADY QUICK-WIT**, passing in hast over the Stage.

**LADY QUICK-WIT**
Follow, follow.

[Enter **MRS WANTON**.

**MRS WANTON**
Call, call, call.

[Enter **MOTHER**.

**MOTHER**
Bring, bring, bring.

[The **MEN** stand in a Maze.

[Enter **FOOL** passing over the Stage.

**FOOL**
Oh the Lord! I am undone, undone.

[The **MEN** stop him.

**CONVERSANT**
What is the matter, Fool?

**FOOL**
I cannot stay to tell you.

**OBSERVER**
But you must.

**FOOL**
If I must, I must.

**CONVERSANT**
Tell me what makes this Hubbub, which seems to distract the Ladies? is the Emperor not well, or the Princess sick?

**FOOL**
The Emperor is well, but will have cause to be sick; and the Princess is sick, and will have cause to be well.

**MODE**
How so?

**FOOL**
Because the Princess has spi'd her Idea, and will marry him, and so will be cured of her Melancholy, and be well; but he is a poor Mariner or Sea-man, and that will make the Emperor sick.

[Enter the **LADIES**, and the **MARINER** passing over the Stage.

**FOOL**
Now you have seen the cause of the uproar, you will let me pass with my fellow-fools.

[Exit **FOOL**.

**CONVERSANT**
Sure the Princess will not Marry this poor fellow.

**OBSERVER**
If she doth, the Court will be Metamorphorsed from a house to a Ship, and the Courtiers to Mariners.

**MODE**
Then we shall sail to some new Plantation.

[Enter **LADY QUICK-WIT**, **LADY SELF-CONCEIT**, **MRS WANTON**.

**MRS WANTON**
As I live, he is a handsom Man.

**LADY SELF-CONCEIT**
But he is a poor mean fellow.

**MRS WANTON**
But a poor mean fellow may be a handsom
Man.

**LADY SELF-CONCEIT**
Not in my opinion.

**LADY QUICK-WIT**

Truly I am of the opinion, that Wealth doth not make Worth.

[Exeunt.

SCENE I

[Enter the **SAILER** leading the **PRINCESS**, who appears well pleased, with the Attendance of **LADIES** and **GENTLEMEN**, and the **FOOL**.

**PRINCESS**
Sir, although the Emperor is at Council, and will not be seen at the present, yet I will entertain you until such time as his Majesty admits you to his Presence.

[The **SAILER** Kisses her Hand.

**FOOL**
They say, Lovers promise much; if so, you are a Lover, for you promise more then you dare perform.

**PRINCESS**
How so?

**FOOL**
You say, you will entertain the Sailer 's Company until the Emperor admits him to his Presence, and if he doth not admit him until to morrow, you must entertain his Company all night.

**PRINCESS**
You are a Knave, Fool.

**FOOL**
But I am not a Lady's Fool.

**PRINCESS**
Come Gentlemen and Ladies, call for Musick, for we will dance until the Emperor rises from Council.

[One calls for Musick.

**PRINCESS**
Sir, can you dance our Country Dances.

**SAILER**
I will do my endeavour, Lady; and if I have not skill for the present, I will learn for the future, if you command me.

[The Musick plays, they all dance, and the SAILER with the PRINCESS; the SAILER dances civilly, gracefully, and with art and skill.

**PRINCESS**
Sir, you want not Art, for you Dance skilfully.

**SAILER**
Lady, I want not Love, and Love works
Miracles.

[They Dance again: At the end of this Dance Enters a **GENTLEMAN**.

**GENTLEMAN**
May it please your Highness, the Emperor desires your Presence.

[The **PRINCESS** whispers to the **SAILER**, he bows and kisses her Hand.

[Exeunt **ALL**.


SCENE II

[Enter all the **MAIDS OF HONOUR**, except **LADY BASHFUL**, and **LADY SELF-CONCEIT**; as also **MONSIEUR CONVERSANT**, **OBSERVER** and **SPEND-ALL**.

**MRS WANTON**
O that we might dance Country Dances to day.

**LADY WAGTAIL**
Why, Monsieur Spend-all makes a Ball to night, are not you one of the invited?

**MRS WANTON**
O yes, but I had forgot the Ball.

**LADY QUICK-WIT**
Why, we are all invited.

[Enter **LADY SELF-CONCEIT**.

**LADY SELF-CONCEIT**
Do you hear the News?

**MRS WANTON**
What News?

**LADY SELF-CONCEIT**
Madamoisel Bashful and the Lord Loyalty are

Married.

**LADY WAGTAIL**
For certain truth do you speak it?

**LADY SELF-CONCEIT**
Of a certain truth 'tis so.

**LADY QUICK-WIT**
Why, the Lord Loyalty was accounted a
Wise Man.

**OBSERVER**
Why, Madam, he is never the less Wise for
Marrying a virtuous sweet Lady.

**LADY QUICK-WIT**
What, not in these troublesome and mutinous
Times.

**OBSERVER**
In all times there was and is Marrying, and giving in Marriage; and those that are Honest are Wise, and it is Honest to Marry, and Wise; for if Men and Women should live in common, it were the way to extinguish Propriety; and where there is no Propriety, there is no Justice; and without Justice a Commonwealth would be dissolved.

**LADY WAGTAIL**
Well, in my opinion he has done very indiscreetly.

**MRS WANTON**
Nay, faith, methinks, he hath done very foolishly.

**LADY SELF-CONCEIT**
In my opinion, she has done as foolishly as he, for he is a ruined man.

**CONVERSANT**
Give me leave to tell you, Ladies, there is never a one of you all who would have refused him, as ruined as he is; but you would have been ambitious and proud to Marry him.

**LADY WAGTAIL**
You are deceived; for I would not Marry him or any other, were he as rich as Pluto.

**MRS WANTON**
Nor I would not Marry, might I have a King.

**LADY QUICK-WIT**
Nor I to have been an Emperess.

**LADY SELF-CONCEIT**
Nor I if I might have been Mistress of the whole
World.

**SPEND-ALL**
Then I perceive, Ladies, you are all resolved to live single lives.

**LADY WAGTAIL**
There is none happy, but those that are Mistresses of themselves.

**LADY QUICK-WIT**
I should never endure to be subject to a Husband.

**MRS WANTON**
I hate Marriage as I hate death.

**LADY SELF-CONCEIT**
I love Freedom, as I love Life.

[Enter **MOTHER**.

**LADY QUICK-WIT**
Mother, do you hear of your Daughter's
Marriage?

**MOTHER**
Yes, and the Princess is very angry at it.

**LADY QUICK-WIT**
She hath reason.

**LADY SELF-CONCEIT**
If I were the Princess, I would make them repent their Marriage.

**LADY WAGTAIL**
Yes faith, I would put water into their Wine.

**OBSERVER**
Lord, Ladies, why should the Princess be angry either with him, or with her, since Marriage is honest, and free for every one to chuse where they please; neither do I see either in Reason or Justice, why either of them should be condemned, since none will suffer, if they be unhappy, but themselves; and I suppose that none here is so ill-natured as to repine at their Felicity.

**LADY SELF-CONCEIT**
Come, pray let us go see how she looks since she is Married.

**MRS WANTON**
Proud, I'le warrant you.

**LADY WAGTAIL**

I dare swear she will carry state now.

**LADY SELF-CONCEIT**

She was proud enough before she was Married, she cannot be much prouder then she was.

**LADY QUICK-WIT**

You say right, for what every body thought was bashfulness and modesty in her, was meerly pride.

[Exeunt **LADIES**, the **MEN** stay.

**OBSERVER**

The Maids of Honour live so happily in the Court, and are so pleased with their several Courtships, as they hate to think of Marriage.

**MODE**

That's because they cannot get Husbands; for Men are afraid to Marry Maids of Honour, because they are so used to Courtships, that they will give leave to be Courted when they are Married; besides, Men think them vain and expensive.

**SPEND-ALL**

They speak so bitterly against Marriage, and all that are Married, as I do verily believe they would not Marry upon any condition.

**MODE**

I will try them whether they will or no, for my own satisfaction.

**OBSERVER**

Which way will you try them? for if you should examine them never so soberly, and gravely, they will never discover their minds so, that you shall know whether they would Marry or not.

**MODE**

Faith, I will offer every one of them a Husband, and try if they will accept of them.

**OBSERVER**

O, they will laugh at you, and scorn you for your offer.

**MODE**

Well, I will try them, let them scorn and laugh as they please.

[Enter **MONSIEUR CONVERSANT**.

**CONVERSANT**

Monsieur Mode, I hear you intend to travel into Foreign Nations.

**MODE**

You hear right, Sir; for I want only travel to make me a compleat Mode-Gallant; whereby, I shall be more graceful in the eyes of the Ladies.

**SPEND-ALL**
But if your Travels be long, you will be less graceful in the eyes of the Ladies, for you will be too old to please their sight; but you want not Mistresses, nor the art of Courtship.

**MODE**
Faith, to tell you the truth, I would travel to see Foreign Beauties; for I am satisfied with the Ladies here in my Native Country.

**OBSERVER**
I hope you have not taken a surfeit of them.

**SPEND-ALL**
Truly I should be glad to have some of his
Leavings.

**CONVERSANT**
It is a sign you are sharp set.

**OBSERVER**
The old Lady has whet his appetite.

**SPEND-ALL**
I confess old Women make wanton young Men.

**CONVERSANT**
Let Monsieur Mode Court your old Lady to cure his surfeit.

**SPEND-ALL**
With all my heart, so he will bequeath me his young Mistresses.

**MODE**
I did instruct you how to Court and gain
Ladies to your Imbracements; but either you are a dull
Scholar, or an unfortunate Courtier.

**SPEND-ALL**
I confess my ill fortune in Courtships; but you may be as unfortunate in Foreign Nations; for though you are A la Mode here in your Native Country, 'tis likely you will be quite out of fashion and language in other Nations.

**CONVERSANT**
For Language, I dare say he will be to learn.

**OBSERVER**
Then how will he Woo a Mistress?

**MODE**

O, Women are best pleased with those they understand least.

**SPEND-ALL**

He knows the humours of Women best, he is so conversant with them; but prithee Mode do not travel until I have learn'd thy Art of Courtship.

**CONVERSANT**

Into what Countries will you travel, Monsieur
Mode?

**MODE**

Into France and Italy; the one to refine my
Habit, the other to refresh my sight with new
Beauties.

**OBSERVER**

Then they must not be cast Courtisans; but let me perswade you to stay at home, and Marry.

**MODE**

No, I will not Marry, to lose my freedom.

**SPEND-ALL**

Faith, and I intend to Marry to take more liberty.

**MODE**

Marriage is a bondage.

**SPEND-ALL**

Not if you Marry a rich old Woman.

**CONVERSANT**

No, for her Riches will supply his wants, and maintain his Mistresses; and her age will be an excuse for his Adulteries.

**MODE**

Faith, Gentlemen, you speak reason; wherefore, I'le go a Wooing to Monsieur Spend-all 's old rich Lady.

**SPEND-ALL**

You will not speed there, for I am aforehand with you; for though you can Court young Women better then I, yet for old Women I go beyond you. But if you chance to Marry a young Woman, I shall willingly change a nights lodging with you.

**MODE**

Are you Married to the old Lady?

**SPEND-ALL**

I must Marry her, which is my grief.

**MODE**
Pray bid us to your Wedding.

**SPEND-ALL**
That I will, and feast you after I am Married,for I shall not be jealous of my Wife, nor afraid you will make me a Cuckold; and I have a desire to invite the young Female Courtiers.

**OBSERVER**
That will make your old Lady jealous; and if she be jealous, when you are just upon the point of Marriage, she may chance to refuse you; wherefore, do not invite them until the next day, when she is past her choice.

**SPEND-ALL**
You say true, and the next day we will Revel.


SCENE III

[Enter **LADY SELF-CONCEIT** and **LADY QUICK-WIT**.

**LADY QUICK-WIT**
The Emperor is highly discontent.

**LADY SELF-CONCEIT**
If he be displeased, he can only be angry with himself; for when the Princess was so Melancholy, that she was ready to die, he did assure her, she should make her own choice of a Husband, and that he would not deny her any one Man in all his Empire.

**LADY QUICK-WIT**
But this Man is not of his Empire, for he is a stranger.

**LADY SELF-CONCEIT**
Faith, it would be but an even Match, whether she did chuse a poor mean Native, or a poor mean Stranger.

[Exeunt.


SCENE IV

[Enter **PRINCESS** and the **SAILER**; the **FOOL** attends them; the **PRINCESS** Weeps.

**SAILER**

Why doth your Highness weep? for if the Emperor your Father be unjust, the Gods will not be so; for they will Crown our honest Loves with Happiness and Blessings.

**PRINCESS**
But Lovers are never happy.

**SAILER**
Believe not so; for true Lovers are always blessed with good success, and those that have ill fortune have not been true Lovers.

[Enter such **MEN** as are proper to deliver the Emperor's pleasure; they speak to the **SAILER**.

**MEN**
Sailer,
The Emperor's pleasure is,
That you immediately go out of his Dominions; for if you be found in any part within such time as may be travel'd to the Sea-side the shortest way, he will cut off your Head.

**SAILER**
Tell the Emperor, I fear not death.

**MEN**
Will not you be gone.

**SAILER**
No, I will stay as long as I can.

**MEN**
But you shall go, since it is the Emperor's pleasure,
That we see you out of his Empire.

**SAILER**
Be gone, and trouble me no more, or I'le beat you out of the Princess's Lodgings.

**MEN**
You beat us, you poor Water-Snake!

**SAILER**
Cupid, thou god of Love, and Mars thou god of War, assist me.

[He falls upon them, and beats them out of the Room; the **PRINCESS** seems to be in a fright.

**SAILER**
A Company of Cowardly Rascals, that have no more Courage then a Flea, that skips at every little motion.

**PRINCESS**
O my dear Love! what will you do?

**SAILER**
Die in your Arms, sweet Mistress.

**PRINCESS**
But you cannot resist the Emperor's Power.

**SAILER**
But I can die in despite of the Emperor's
Power.

**PRINCESS**
But your death will be my death.

**SAILER**
Say not so; for those words will beget such a belief, as to make me a Coward, which is more terrible to me then death; for in death lives Rest, but in a Coward lives Infamy.

**PRINCESS**
But pray consider, if you will yield to depart out of the Empire, I may find means to depart with you, or to follow you.

**SAILER**
Death is more Honourable then to fly from any misfortune; and though I love you better then my Soul, yet I had rather die then fly.

**PRINCESS**
But by your willing death, you will become a cruel murderer, not only to your self, but me.

**SAILER**
Die you must, my dear Mistress, so must I.

**PRINCESS**
Heaven grant that in one Grave we both may lie.

**FOOL**
Shed no more tears, nor talk of Graves; for if you will absolutely be ruled by me, if I be not too hard for the Emperor, and all his Councels, hang me when you are Emperess, which you must be; for the Power and Title comes from your Mother, not from your Father.

**PRINCESS**
Tell me how?

**FOOL**
Nay faith, a Fool must have some time for contrivance, as well as wise States-Men.

[Exeunt.

[Enter **MONSIEUR MODE**, and **LADY QUICK-WIT**.

**MODE**
Lady, there is one of my Acquaintance, that desires a Wife; but he may desire long enough, for I think none will have him for a Husband.

**LADY QUICK-WIT**
Why?

**MODE**
Why! he is the most deformed Man that ever was seen.

**LADY QUICK-WIT**
Well, if I were to chuse a Husband, I would never chuse a handsom Man; for their Beauty makes them so self-conceited, that they regard not their Wives; besides, they seem, and are for the most part, effeminate, which I hate; wherefore, for my part, I would chuse an ill-favoured Man, and the more ill-favoured he were, the better I should like him, as looking more Masculine.

**MODE**
O! but that's not all, Madam; for his Nature and Disposition is according to his Person; the one as evil, as the other ill-favour'd.

**LADY QUICK-WIT**
O Sir, such a man I could love with all my heart; for a surly Nature seems Heroick; when as such men as have sweet Dispositions, and gentle Natures, which is to be soft and facil, are Fools; and I would not marry a Fool for any thing in the world.

**MODE**
But Madam, let me tell you, He is none of the wisest.

**LADY QUICK-WIT**
Nay, Sir, mistake me not; for I would not have him a very wise man, lest he should condemn me as a Fool, but an indifferent understanding I like best.

**MODE**
Why, then this man would be a fit Husband for you.

**LADY QUICK-WIT**
The fittest in the World; Good Monsieur
Mode speak for me, and I shall think my self obliged to you.

**MODE**

I shall motion you, Lady.

[Exit **LADY QUICK-WIT**.

[Enter **LADY SELF-CONCEIT**.

**MODE**
Madam, there is a Gentleman, an Acquaintance of mine, which intreated me to ask you, whether you would please to accept of him for a Husband, if he should offer himself to you; he is loth to have a personal denial, wherefore he would not make his addresses himself, unless he had an assurance you would entertain him.

**LADY SELF-CONCEIT**
Pray Sir, what manner of man is he?

**MODE**
Faith Lady, I cannot much commend either his Person, or Parts, Humour, or Disposition; but he has a Competent Fortune, not so much, as to maintain a Wife gallantly, but decently.

**LADY SELF-CONCEIT**
Why, that's as much as I desire; more would be but an unnecessary superfluity; as for Person, I regard not the outward Shape; and for his Humour and Disposition, I shall alter those when we are married; and truly Sir, I think my self much obliged to you, for mentioning the man unto me.

**MODE**
Your Servant Lady.

**LADY SELF-CONCEIT**
Yours, Monsieur Mode.

[Exit **LADY SELF-CONCEIT**.

[Enter **MRS WANTON**.

**MODE**
Lady, I am tyred with the importunity of a Gentleman, that will not let me rest in quiet, until I have inform'd you of his Affections to you, and for you.

**MRS WANTON**
Who is he?

**MODE**
Nay, he must be unknown, until he know whether you will accept of him; but in truth, my Conscience bids me perswade you against him; indeed I would not have mention'd him, but that he will not let me rest, till I have told you his desires.

**MRS WANTON**
What manner of Man is he? and what Estate has he? and of what Qualitiy is he?

**MODE**

He is a Gentleman, and as for his Person, tospeak truth, he is a very Handsom man, as any is, but he is not worth a Denier, a very Shark for his living.

**MRS WANTON**

I marry Sir, give me a Man that lives by his wits; for every Fool can tell how to live, if he be rich; besides, I had rather enjoy Beauty, then Wealth, with a Husband.

**MODE**

O, but that's not all, Madam; for he is a very deboist Man; he Drinks, and Whores, and Games.

**MRS WANTON**

Marriage will reclaim him.

**MODE**

But he has got such a Habit of Debauchery, that 'tis to be fear'd, he will never be reclaimed.

**MRS WANTON**

The truth of it is, I would chuse a deboist Man for a Husband sooner then a Temperate Man; for his several Debaucheries will be my several Pastimes; besides, I shall have his Company but sometimes, which will make him appear to me fresh and new; whereas, a Stoical and Temperate Husband, will tire me out with his continual Company, being always at home, or else he would restrain me with his Moral Discipline.

**MODE**

But there is another reason, that may disswade you from him.

**MRS WANTON**

What's that?

**MODE**

Why, 'tis said, he has the French Pox, and I believe you will not venture on that Disease.

**MRS WANTON**

I am of so healthful a Constitution, I fear no Disease; besides, he is not a Courtly nor well-bred Man, that has not a spice of that Disease; and the truth is, I should account that Man uncivil, and not a Gentleman, but a meer dull Clown that were free thereof, and sound there-from; for the compleatest Gentlemen are ever under the Arrest of that Disease; wherefore, Sir, to release you of his importunity, tell him from me, I shall not refuse him, but willingly accept of him.

**MODE**

I shall Madam.

[Exeunt.

[Enter **LADY WAGTAIL**, **LADY SELF-CONCEIT**, and **MRS WANTON**.

**LADY WAGTAIL**
LORD! Self-conceit, I have not seen you never since the night before the last night!

**LADY SELF-CONCEIT**
You might have seen me if you had been so kind as to come to my Lodging, for I lay a bed all yesterday, by reason I had a great many to come to Visit me, and they were Men of Quality.

**LADY WAGTAIL**
Faith, I could not come, by reason Monsieur Malicious was going over, to whom you know, I have intrusted all my affairs, so as I was dispatching some business with him.

**LADY SELF-CONCEIT**
But I will never forgive my friend Wanton, that she would not come with the Lords and Gentlemen to visit me.

**MRS WANTON**
Faith, I could not come; for my Chamber-fellow and I, both of us, did bath yesterday, and there came in two or three Gentlemen whilst we were in the Bath,and stay'd talking so long with us that I have catch'd Cold.

**LADY SELF-CONCEIT**
Lord! did Madamoisel Supple Bath again yesterday! why she bathed but the day before; for a Gentleman told me, that Madam Liberty was in the Bath, and when she went out, then she went into Madamoisel Supple 's Bed to warm and dry her self, and Mr. Amorous entertain'd her whilst she lay there, and Madamoisel Supple, as soon as Madamoisel Liberty went out of the Bath, went into it; and by that time that Madamoisel Liberty rose out of the bed, Madamoisel Supple was ready to enter into it, and then Mr. Break-jest did entertain her with pleasant Discourses.

**MRS WANTON**
Certainly, Bathing is very wholsome.

**LADY SELF-CONCEIT**
But let me tell you, Wanton, that often Bathing weakens very much.

[Exeunt **MRS WANTON** and **LADY SELF-CONCEIT**.

[**LADY WAGTAIL** Sola, Enter to her **MODE**.

**LADY WAGTAIL**
Monsieur Mode, I have watch'd for an opportunity to speak to you alone these two or three days.

**MODE**
To me, sweet Lady! what is it you would say?

**LADY WAGTAIL**
'Tis this; I hear you are acquainted with a Man, who is very rich and unmarried, and 'tis reported he will marry a Wife of your chusing; and Sir, I shall not be ungrateful, if you will chuse me for his Wife.

**MODE**
'Tis true, I am acquainted with such a Man,who is very rich, but he is a very Fool; the truth is, the next degree to a Changeling.

**LADY WAGTAIL**
I like that the better, for so I may govern him and his Estate.

**MODE**
Nay, Lady, let me inform you, that though he be a Fool, yet he is a covetous and self-conceited Fool, neither to be ruled nor wrought upon, nor yet to be perswaded to any thing, but what he himself likes best.

**LADY WAGTAIL**
However Sir, I shall gain a respect and esteem in the World by the Reputation of his Wealth; wherefore, good Monsieur Mode, let me intreat you to prefer me to his good liking.

**MODE**
I shall do my endeavour, Lady.

[Exit **LADY WAGTAIL**.

[Enter **OBSERVER** to **MODE**.

**OBSERVER**
The Sailer is gone to Prison, and the Princess confin'd to her Chamber.

**MODE**
I am sorry for the Princess's restraint.

[Exeunt.


SCENE III

[Enter **SAILER**: as in a Prison, Manicled with Chains.

**SAILER**
You Heav'nly Powers, do you her life secure,
Show'r blessings on her Life, and let her Name
Be glorious to Posterity and Fame:
But I profane, thou art a Deitie;
Wherefore my Prayers, I'le direct to thee:
Thou Goddess know'st, what torments I do feel,

My life is wrack'd upon ill-fortune's wheel.
O! do not break my heart, thou Heav'nly Power,
For 'tis thy own Idea's onely Tower;
For when I dye, where will thy Mansion be?
In every Heart and Head that thinks of thee:
Then let me die in peace, for thou wilt reign
In every Soul, as well as every Brain.

[Exeunt.


SCENE IV

[Enter **JAYLOR** and **FOOL**.

**FOOL**
Master Jaylor?

**JAYLOR**
What say you, Mr. Fool?

**FOOL**
Will you take a Fool's Counsel?

**JAYLOR**
No by my Faith.

**FOOL**
Then by my Faith,
I'le prove you a Fool; for my Counsel is,
To let the Sailer escape.

**JAYLOR**
So I shall be hang'd my self.

**FOOL**
That is uncertain; but if the Sailer suffers, you are sure to be hang'd.

**JAYLOR**
How so?

**FOOL**
Why you know the Princess must be Emperess,because that Dignity comes by her Mother; and the Emperor is but Emperor during life, and so upon Courtesie; and when the Princess is Emperess, she will be sure to hang you, and not only hang you, but ruine all your Posterity.

**JAYLOR**

Go, go, you talk like a Fool as you are! I will be an honest Jaylor, and not betray my Prisoners.

**FOOL**
Not betray your Prisoners, say you! consider well, lest you betray your self.

[Exit **FOOL**, **JAYLER** Solus.

**JAYLOR**
This Fool has a notable Wit.

[Exit.


SCENE V

[Enter **MRS WANTON**, **LADY WAGTAIL**, **LADY SELF-CONCEIT**, and **QUICK-WIT**.

**LADY WANTON**
WHEN did you see Monsieur Mode?

**LADY WAGTAIL**
I have not seen him these two days.

**LADY SELF-CONCEIT**
Nor I.

**LADY QUICK-WIT**
Nor I.

**MRS WANTON**
I fear he is sick.

**LADY WAGTAIL**
I hope in God, not.

**LADY SELF-CONCEIT**
Pray Heav'n grant he be in health.

**LADY QUICK-WIT**
Amen; for he is one of the civillest persons I know.

**MRS WANTON**
Indeed he is an obliging person.

**LADY WAGTAIL**
He is a gallant Man.

**LADY SELF-CONCEIT**
The truth is, he has not his equal.

[Enter **CONVERSANT**.

**CONVERSANT**
Ladies, what happy Man is he that you are praising.

**LADY SELF-CONCEIT**
Why, Monsieur Mode?

**LADY WAGTAIL**
He is a Man that may be a Sample to all Men.

**LADY QUICK-WIT**
There is none can parallel him.

**MRS WANTON**
He is worth more then praise can give him.

**CONVERSANT**
He cannot chuse but prosper in his Travels, when he is so highly praised by a Company of Beautiful Ladies.

**MRS WANTON**
In his Travels! why whither is he gone?

**CONVERSANT**
Into Italy; and the Company he is gone with, went on such a sudden, as he had no time to come and kiss your hands, and take his leave; but he has sent me to make his excuse, and beg his pardon, although he could not help it, unless he should have lost those Conveniences he has by going in the Company of such as can speak the Language, which he cannot.

**LADY QUICK-WIT**
Pray speak no more of him, for it is no matter whither he is gone, since he has no more Civility.

**LADY SELF-CONCEIT**
Never was there such an act done by a Gentleman, as to go not only out of the Town, but the Kingdom, and never take his leave of us.

**MRS WANTON**
Faith, he has shewn himself what he is, a
Clown.

**LADY WAGTAIL**
A meer Booby.

**LADY SELF-CONCEIT**

A Boor.

**LADY QUICK-WIT**
Indeed by his behaviour to us he seems not to be a Gentleman.

**MRS WANTON**
One might have easily judged what he was, if any would have taken the pains to consider him.

**LADY WAGTAIL**
I despise such a man.

**LADY SELF-CONCEIT**
I hate such a man.

**MRS WANTON**
I abhor him.

**CONVERSANT**
Ladies, I perceive our Sex is very unhappy, for you will love and hate us in a minute, and praise and dispraise us in one breath.

**LADIES**
We have reason.

[Enter **SPEND-ALL**, **CONVERSANT**, **OBSERVER**, and the **LADIES**.

**SPEND-ALL**
Ladies I have ask'd the Princess leave, that you, Her Maids, should honour me with your Presence at my Marriage Feast.

**LADY SELF-CONCEIT**
Are you Married?

**SPEND-ALL**
Yes.

**LADY QUICK-WIT**
What fair Lady, have you Married?

**SPEND-ALL**
Madam, my condition perswaded me to chuse a fair Fortune, rather then a fair Face; but what she wants in Beauty, she has in age, I should have said in Wealth.

**LADY QUICK-WIT**
It is a sign her Age is in your mind, more then her Wealth, that your tongue was so ready to speak it.

**LADY WAGTAIL**
But if your Lady be old, we that are young, shall hardly be welcom.

[Enter **MODE**.

**MRS WANTON**
Lord, Monsieur Mode, I thought you had been gone to Travel.

**MODE**
No, that design is alter'd; for I intend now to stay, and marry a rich old Lady too.

**LADY SELF-CONCEIT**
If all the young Gallants marry old Women,
What shall we young Women do for Husbands?

**MODE**
It were great pity, and not to be suffred, that young Women should marry whil'st their Beauty doth last; but they should live unmarried, to be Mistresses to command Men, and not made slaves to obey, as Wives are.

**LADY QUICK-WIT**
The best for young Women, is to marry ancient Men, for so we shall be Vertuous Mistresses to wise men in a married condition and life.

**CONVERSANT**
But Lady, all the younger sort of Men, are not so necessitated through their lavish expences, to marry for Riches; for I am not so vain, nor poor, but I may marry for Beauty, and not any Beauty pleaseth me so well as yours.

**LADY QUICK-WIT**
I had rather be married for my Wit, then for my Beauty.

**CONVERSANT**
That man is happy, Lady, that can have a
Wife with both.

**LADY SELF-CONCEIT**
This is just according to the Old Saying,
That one Wedding makes two.

**OBSERVER**
And if you please Madam, these two Weddings shall be the cause of a third.

**LADY SELF-CONCEIT**
Let us see, how the married Couples agree first.

**MODE**
We will have no particular Wooing, but all shall be in common; otherwise, our meeting will be dull, and our mirth out of tune.

**MRS WANTON**
You say right, Monsieur Mode, for the fiddle-string of Mirth will be broken; but let us go and rejoyce with Mr. Spend-all, and dance and feast, as a Thanksgiving to Fortune for her favours to him.

**SPEND-ALL**
The greatest favour that Fortune can give me, is, to be honoured with your Company; and if you please to lead the way, the rest will follow.

[He sighs.

Ha! these Marriages spoile all Amorous
Courtships.

[Exeunt **OMNES**, each leading his **MISTRESS**.


SCENE VI

[Enter **FOOL**, and the **SAILER** as in a Prison.

**FOOL**
Master Sailer, the Princess has sent to know of you, whether you be dead?

**SAILER**
In her absence I am dead to all Happiness, for
I have no joys of life.

**FOOL**
Then I shall tell her you are dead.

**SAILER**
You may tell her I am worse then dead; for I am miserable, wanting her Company, and misery is worse then death.

**FOOL**
Pray God I remember all this; viz. Absence,
Happiness, Joys, Life, Dead, Miserable, Misery, and
Death.

[Exeunt.


SCENE VII

[Enter **PRINCESS** alone, Musing; Enter **FOOL** to her.

**FOOL**

O Lady! Lady! the Sailer 's dead.

[She falls into a passion as distracted, then speaks.

**PRINCESS**

Make me a Ship to sail! up high to Heav'n,
Where I may swim through all the Planets Seven;
Not to find Gold or Silver, such base dross,
But my dear Love and Lover; which rich loss
Is worth more then the World: Or, make a Boat,
That I may thorough the dark: Stygian float
To the Elysium, there to meet my Dear,
Where I shall neither State nor Father fear:
Or else, you Gods, cast me so low and deep,
Without a Dream I may for ever sleep.

[The **FOOL** Laughs.

**FOOL**

Ha, ha, ha, Dreams, Ships and Water has been your ruine.

**PRINCESS**

You Villain, do you laugh at my misery?

[She gives him a Box of the Ear.

**FOOL**

O, do not beat me, your Sailer 's alive yet.

**PRINCESS**

Did not you tell me he was dead?

**FOOL**

Yes, but I did not tell you his Body is dead, but his Joys are dead.

**PRINCESS**

Is he alive then?

**FOOL**

He is alive, but talks as madly, I dare not say, as foolishly as you do.

[Exeunt.

[A Scaffold and Block for one to be beheaded. Enter the **GUARD**, **JAYLOR** and **PRISONER**; as also a **GRAVE MAN**, as his Father; the **PEOPLE** staring upon them. The **PRISONER** being upon the Scaffold, bows down gracefully to the Assembly, and then speaks thus.

## SAILER
Worthy Spectators, although I am a Stranger by Birth, yet I am as a Native, being a loving Subject, and humble servant of your Soveraign the Princess; but Fortune which takes more delight in Variety, then Justice, has not only toss'd me from Climate to Climate, and Nation to Nation, but from Happiness to Misery, from Misery to Happiness, and from Happiness to Misery again; and yet my life will end happily; for I shall be a Sacrifice on the Altar of Love, which is such an Honour, that not any worthy person would refuse or repine at; for all true Lovers will bear up my Hearse with Sighs, cover it with Tears, and intomb me in their Memory.

[Upon this Speech the **PEOPLE** begin to murmur; then the **GRAVE MAN** steps up.

## GRAVE MAN
Worthy Spectators, This Person which is here ready to die for Love, (yet not for the Love you imagine) is no wayes capable of Marrying your Princess; for this Person is not only a Woman, but a Princess her self; being Daughter to the Emperor of Persia, who for Love hath wilfully banished her self from her Father's Court and Empire: My Wife was her Governness, God rest her Soul; she being dead, and I her Guardian, did love this Princess as my own Child; and knowing her design was not to be alter'd, have attended her, both in her Disguise and Travels; but your Princess imagining her a Man, being in Mans Clothes, has unfortunately fallen in Love with her, which has been the cause both of our trouble and discovery: But I hope this Nation is more just then to murder an innocent Princess, that has not committed any fault either to the People or their Soveraign.

## THE PEOPLE [Calling out]
Long live the Princess, remove her, and conveigh her to the Emperor.

SCENE IX

[Enter **CONVERSANT** and **OBSERVER**, with **LADY QUICK-WIT**, and **LADY SELF-CONCEIT**.

## CONVERSANT
Lord, they say, there's such a noise about the Place where the Sailer should be executed, as it's fear'd there will be some mutiny or uproar amongst the People.

## LADY QUICK-WIT
Faith, the Emperor would be justly served, if there were a Rebellion against him, so it might not be a danger to his Daughter.

## LADY SELF-CONCEIT
I did not believe the Princess would be so patient as she is.

## OBSERVER
O, the less anger she shews the more malice is inclos'd.

**LADY QUICK-WIT**
She is too Vertuous to bear malice to her
Father.

**CONVERSANT**
But it is said, Love and Ambition know no
Kindred.

[Enter **MODE**.

**MODE**
Ladies, yonder is the strangest accident that ever was.

**LADY SELF-CONCEIT**
Lord! what strange accident?

**MODE**
The Sailer is prov'd a Woman, and the Woman is proved a Princess, Daughter to the Persian Emperor.

**OBSERVER**
What, has the Princess been in Love with a
Woman?

**MODE**
Yes.

**LADY QUICK-WIT**
Pray, Monsieur Mode, tell us how she was known to be a Woman, and who made the discovery?

**MODE**
Why thus it was. When this Lady in Sailer 's Clothes was mounted on the Scaffold, and had made a very witty Speech; there steps up an ancient Man, and made a Speech, wherein, he told the People, She was a Woman, and Daughter to the Emperor of Persia, and that he was a Noble Man of Persia, who had travel'd with her; for by reason his Wife, who was dead, had been Governess to the Lady, he having no Children, was as fond of the Princess, as if she had been his own Child; and seeing her pine away for Love, and her beloved gone, or rather banished the Empire, she resolving to follow him, and to endeavour to find him, and that all his Perswasions could not prevail, he (although in years) did travel with her, to be both her Guide, Counsellor and Guardian. Whereupon, all the People shouted for Joy, and cried out, Carry her to the Emperor, Carry her to the Emperor; So both she and the old Man are carried before the Emperor, but what will be the Event, I cannot tell.

**LADY SELF-CONCEIT**
For God's sake, Quick-wit, let us go to the Princess, and tell her this.

**LADY QUICK-WIT**
We shall not need, for she will have News of it before we come, and will be as sad that the Sailer is a Woman, as if he had been hang'd.

[Enter **SPEND-ALL**.

**SPEND-ALL**
The Sailer is prov'd a Woman.

**CONVERSANT**
That we have heard.

**SPEND-ALL**
But you have not heard that she has been with the Emperor, and that he seems to be in Love with her in her Sailer 's Clothes.

**OBSERVER**
It would be a strange cross Caper, if he should marry the Sailer, for whom his Daughter was dying, and mad for love.

**SPEND-ALL**
Certainly, he seem'd strangely to alter with her Presence.

**LADY SELF-CONCEIT**
Come Quick-wit, let us go and see how our
Lady the Princess takes this.

[Exeunt **LADIES**, **MEN** Solus.

**OBSERVER**
But can the Emperor be so suddenly in Love?

**SPEND-ALL**
Love makes no stay, nor takes Counsel.

[Exeunt.


SCENE X

Enter **PRINCESS** and the **LADIES**.

**LADY QUICK-WIT**
But Madam, can your Highness be well pleas'd, that the Sailer is prov'd a Woman, and that the Emperor should love her so, as to profess, he will Marry her if she agree?

**PRINCESS**
Yes; for though the Emperor my Father was unjust to me, I cannot, nor never shall be undutiful to him.

**LADY SELF-CONCEIT**

But is your Melancholy passion of Love past?

**PRINCESS**
My Melancholy is past, but not my Love; for that will live so long as I shall live, and will remain pure in my Soul, when my body is dead and turn'd to dust.

**LADY QUICK-WIT**
Your Highness is a miracle of duty and constancy in Love, although the last is but a Dream.

**PRINCESS**
Many Dreams are Prophetical.

[Exeunt.

ACT V

SCENE I

[Enter the **MOTHER** of the Maids, Enter also **MODE** and **SPEND-ALL**.

**SPEND-ALL**
Have you heard the News?

**MODE**
What News?

**SPEND-ALL**
Why, the Sailer that was a Man, and the Man that was proved a Lady, and the Lady a Princess, is now proved no Lady, but is a Man again, and a Sailer.

**MOTHER**
How so?

**SPEND-ALL**
How so? why even as the Man that could change himself into a Wolf, and from a Wolf into a Man again; so the Sailer has the art to make himself a Man, or Woman when he pleases.

**MODE**
I would he could teach all the Court this art.

**MOTHER**
The gods forbid; for if all you Gentlemen should be Women, what would my pritty birds do for Courtly Servants.

**SPEND-ALL**

Why, they might convert themselves into Men, and then there would be a better agreement amongst us; for when we are Women, we shall be kinder to them, when they are Men, then they are to us now they are Women.

**MODE**
But what would your old Lady do, if you were a Woman?

**SPEND-ALL**
Faith, as well as she doth now.

**MODE**
But let us leave our talking, and go to the
Sailer, to learn this Art.

SCENE II

[Enter the **PRINCESS** and the **SAILER** in a Prince's Habit, Enter also the **FOOL**.

**SAILER**
My sweet and dear Mistress, what will you do?
Shall I have no fruition, but still woo?

**PRINCESS**
My noble Love and Servant give me leave,
That I in sport my Father may deceive.

**FOOL**
God's-body, in the time you deceive your
Father, you deceive your self; for he will take his pleasure before you.

**SAILER**
Madam, the Fool speaks truth.

**PRINCESS**
Yes, according to appetite, but not according to chast love.

**FOOL**
Lady, you speak extravagantly, talking of Chast Love, when as never Lover was Chast, for they commit Adultery either in Mind or Body.

**PRINCESS**
I will have you whipt, if you disgrace pure
Love with the name of Adultery.

**FOOL**

You are not a fit Judge, being a Woman; but I will have the Prince my Judge: Sir, do not I deserve a reward for all my good service, had you been so as you are, had not I play'd my part?

**SAILER**
I grant it, and will plead in your behalf.

**PRINCESS**
I speak not against your good service, but your foolish arguments.

**FOOL**
They are doubly wise that can speak well, and do well; but now I will give you Politick Counsel: But first, you must give me Lands; secondly, Moneys; thirdly, you must give me a great Office; and lastly, you must make me a great Lord.

**PRINCESS**
A great Fool, you mean.

**FOOL**
I am that without your making.

**PRINCESS**
But where is the Politick Counsel you would give me?

**FOOL**
I marry, there is the business; the Counsel is, That first the Prince must declare himself, then you may Marry, and then whining Love will abate, and then with God's blessing you may soon come to disagree.

**PRINCESS**
And you are a Knave truly.

**SAILER**
Mistress, I do approve of the Fool's Counsel, as to make my self known to the Emperor; but the way or manner how, is not consider'd as yet.

**FOOL**
I have thought of that too, for your Twin Sister who is as like you as a Pea to a Pea, (whom with my Rhetorick I got the Jaylor to take your place and habit in prison) is now the Emperor's admired Mistress, and he dotes as much on her, as the Princess on you; and if you discover your self to the Emperor, he would be a joyful Man, for now he is afraid to Marry, fearing to displease the Princess; but hoping the Princess will consent to his Marriage if he consent to hers, it will make an even case, and both will be pleased.

**SAILER**
Well Fool, for once your Counsel shall take place.


SCENE III

[Enter **MOTHER** of the Maids, **LADY QUICK-WIT**, and **LADY SELF-CONSEIT**.

**MOTHER**
Well, Ladies, you're obliged to me.

**LADY QUICK-WIT**
For what?

**MOTHER**
For speaking a good word to your Lovers, Mr. Conversant, and Mr. Observer; for if it had not been for me, they would not have Married you.

**LADY SELF-CONCEIT**
You speak in our behalf! why, you cannot speak two words of sense in any Cause.

**LADY QUICK-WIT**
If you have such a powerful Perswasion, why do not you get your other Daughters, Wanton and Wagtail, Husbands?

**MOTHER**
Why so, I shall when their Lovers Wives are dead, and in the mean time they please themselves.

[Enter **CONVERSANT** and **OBSERVER**.

**LADY QUICK-WIT**
Servant, the Mother says, that her Rhetorick and Friendship hath perswaded you to Marry us.

**CONVERSANT**
Your Merit, not her Rhetorick or Friendship, could prevail with us.

**OBSERVER**
Faith, Mother, your Rhetorick would rather lose a Cause, then obtain a Suit.

[Enter **MRS WANTON**.

**MRS WANTON**
Do you hear the News?

**LADY QUICK-WIT**
What News?

**MRS WANTON**
Why, the Sailer is proved a Prince.

**LADY SELF-CONCEIT**
What Prince?

**MRS WANTON**
The Emperor of Persia 's younger Son, who was stollen away by a Noble Man of Persia, with his Sister, they being both Twins, and the Emperor being fond of this Son, his elder Son (this Prince's Brother) designed to destroy him; which the Noble Man perceiving, put himself and the two Princes to the trust of a Master of a Ship of this Empire, and disguised them both as Sailers; and when the Prince was to be beheaded, the Fool did corrupt the Jaylor to take the Sisterin the Room of her Brother, and by that means they were both saved.

[Enter **LADY WAGTAIL**.

**LADY WAGTAIL**
There's such Mirth and Joy with the Emperor and Princess, as never was the like, through the mistake between the Prince, and the Princess his Sister.

[Enter a **GENTLEMAN**.

**GENTLEMAN**
Gentlemen and Ladies, you must all prepare for the solemnity of the Marriage of the Prince of Persia, and our Princess.

**CONVERSANT**
Doth not the Emperor Marry the Princess of
Persia?

**GENTLEMAN**
Yes, but that Marriage will be more private.

**CONSERVANT**
Then Ladies, it will be our Duties, if the Emperor and the Princess will give leave,
That we accompany
the Prince and Princess Bridals, with ours.

**LADY SELF-CONCEIT**
I shall agree.

**LADY QUICK-WIT**
And so shall I.

SCENE IV

[Enter **FOOL** and his **LOVE**.

**FOOL**
Come, the Princess has given leave, that we shall Marry when she Marries; but you must wash your face and hands very clean.

**MAID**

But washing will not make them white.

**FOOL**

That is true; for water or any thing else cannot change their Natural Colour, but a pair of white Gloves will hide your black hands, and a Mask will hide your foul Face; for you shall appear at the Wedding as a Mascarado.

**MAID**

O the Lord! I shall fright the Princess.

**FOOL**

I pray God you do not fright me, and 'tis no matter for frighting the Princess, for she has been used to be frighted of late days.

[Exeunt.

SCENE V

Enter **PRINCESS** as a Bride, and the **PRINCE** as a Bridegroom sitting under a State.

Enter also **CONVERSANT** and **QUICK-WIT**, **OBSERVER** and **LADY SELF-CONCEIT**, as Brides and Bridegrooms, and all the **REST** of the Court.

Then the **PRINCE**, and **PRINCESS** and the rest of the **COMPANY**, dance a Ball after the French fashion; and after this there is an Anti-Mask presented to the **PRINCE** and **PRINCESS**.

MARGARET CAVENDISH – A CONCISE BIBLIOGRAPHY

Philosophical Fancies (1653)
Poems and Fancies (1653)
Philosophical and Physical Opinions (1655)
Nature's Pictures drawn by Fancie's Pencil to the Life (1656)
The World's Olio (1655)
Playes, (1662) folio, containing twenty-one plays including
Loves Adventures
The Several Wits
Youths Glory, and Deaths Banquet
The Lady Contemplation
Wits Cabal
The Unnatural Tragedy
The Public Wooing
The Matrimonial Trouble
Nature's Three Daughters (Beauty, Love and Wit) Part I & Part II

The Religious
The Comical Hash
Bell in Campo
A Comedy of the Apocryphal Ladies
The Female Academy
Plays never before printed (1668), containing five plays.
The Sociable Companions, or the Female Wits
The Presence
The Bridals
The Convent of Pleasure
A Piece of a Play
Orations of Divers Sorts (1662)
Philosophical Letters, or Modest Reflections upon some Opinions in Natural Philosophy maintained by several learned authors of the age (1664)
CCXI Sociable Letters (1664)
Observations upon Experimental Philosophy & Description of a New World (1666)
The Blazing World (1666)
The Life of William Cavendish, Duke, Marquis, and Earl of Newcastle, Earl of Ogle, Viscount Mansfield, and Baron of Bolsover, of Ogle, Bothal, and Hepple, &c. (1667)
Grounds of Natural Philosophy (1668)

www.ingramcontent.com/pod-product-compliance
Lightning Source LLC
Chambersburg PA
CBHW021938040426

42448CB00008B/1134